T0243927

MY LIFE
IN
SEVENTEEN
BOOKS

A LITERARY MEMOIR

JON M. SWEENEY

MONKFISH
RHINEBECK, NEW YORK

Hardcover ISBN 978-1-958972-31-1
eBook ISBN 978-1-958972-32-8

Library of Congress Cataloging-in-Publication Data

Names: Sweeney, Jon M., 1967- author.
Title: My life in seventeen books : a literary memoir / Jon M. Sweeney.
Description: Rhinebeck, New York : Monkfish Book Publishing Company, 2024.
  | Includes bibliographical references and index.
Identifiers: LCCN 2023037430 (print) | LCCN 2023037431 (ebook) | ISBN
  9781958972311 (hardback) | ISBN 9781958972328 (ebook)
Subjects: LCSH: Sweeney, Jon M., 1967---Books and reading. | Books and
  reading--United States. | Books and reading--Psychological aspects. |
  Book industries and trade--United States--Biography. | LCGFT:
  Autobiographies.
Classification: LCC Z1003.2 S96 2011 (print) | LCC Z1003.2 (ebook) | DDC
  381/.45002092 [B]--dc23/eng/20231023
LC record available at https://lccn.loc.gov/2023037430
LC ebook record available at https://lccn.loc.gov/2023037431

Book and cover design by Colin Rolfe

Monkfish Book Publishing Company
22 East Market Street, Suite 304
Rhinebeck, New York 12572
(845) 876-4861
monkfishpublishing.com

Printed in Canada

Remembering Don Dayton, who taught me to scour a bookstore in Chicago, and Tom Loome, who created a paradise in Stillwater.

"Once you do away with the idea of people as fixed, static entities, then you see that people can change, and there is hope."
—bell hooks, *Ain't I a Woman*

"They carried all they could bear, and then some, including a silent awe for the terrible power of the things they carried."
—Tim O'Brien, *The Things They Carried*

CONTENTS

PROLOGUE

These are not my favorite books, nor the ones that changed my mind more than others. These are the seventeen that, most of all, I've carried.

What does it mean to carry a book? I've spent two years pondering this question, and I'm still unsure. Nor am I certain if I have carried these or they have in fact carried me. It's not a question of lifting, transporting, or supporting a bound volume from one place to another. We do that all the time without it being special. Not a single book I was required to carry in college is mentioned here. No, the sort of carrying to which these interrelated essays refer is more the transitive verb kind, the way that one adopts something, or resolves to do something—for instance, the way a committee or court might carry a motion. There is also the intransitive sort of carrying, which applies to some books in my life as well: I am transmitted, the way that the sound of church bells ringing in a city might carry for miles. With bells, this makes good sense, but this wouldn't and couldn't happen with books without some sort of magic, kismet, or enchantment, and with just the right coalescence of person and situation: the ideal moment. These chapters are all about those moments when both the time and the book being carried have been sacred.

I realize not everyone feels it necessary to identify bookish influences in their lives, and I know that there are fewer of us than ever who do. Less than half of adults read just one book in a given year—so if you're still reading, know that you are among a precious few.

Technological developments have caused bookish people, even, to reduce our habit. It has begun to happen to me. We're in thrall to another medium, which is a century old, but now portable, in our pockets and available whenever we demand it. In the thirty minutes I have at the end of each day to be quiet, when I used to read one of several books I was in the thick of, I now often turn to video on a screen. Five hundred years ago, when movable type was invented, people were captivated by printed books in ways that terrified the upholders of every older way of transmitting knowledge and wisdom (oral storytelling, most of all—or the church, according to the priest in Victor Hugo's *Notre-Dame of Paris*). It is while this latest cultural shift is underway, and my attention to books is already not what it once was, that feels like the right time to record what books have meant to me. What they have done for me. I may even look back on this as an exercise of recording what was meaningful, realizing that I may not be able to fully understand it in the future. I write like a man short on time, with the beginning signs of memory loss.

I write for everyone who still looks to bookshelves and cracks open volumes with the expectation that *this next one ... just might ... change my life*. I am that foolish still. Will never lose that optimism for what a book can do.

It works best, in my experience, when the book is old and worn. The English essayist and critic William Hazlitt wrote two centuries ago, "I hate to read new books. There are twenty or thirty volumes that I have read over and over again, and these are the only ones that I have any desire to ever read at all." If it weren't for the fact that I've made my living editing, publishing, marketing, and writing books that are new, I'd say that I agree.

I also know that those of us still influenced by books and authors are usually less prone to influences than those who lean on the words of entertainers, gurus, and celebrities. Book people tend to choose fewer gods, and then discerningly and discriminately. Mine sit quietly on shelves. Which is why when I see a book's descriptive blurb include a marketer's declaration that it's "compulsively readable" I put it back on the display where I found it. No thank you. Not interested in exaggeration when it comes to books. If you find anything compulsively readable you should see a therapist. Even so, the English writer R.H. (Hugh) Benson wrote more than a century ago to a novelist he had never met to tell him that one of his novels was "among the three books from which I never wish to be separated." This I understand. This memoir is my collection of seventeen.

I was in fact schooled in the euphemistic and exaggerated art of copywriting for book jackets. "Highly sought after," "widely regarded," and "recognized as an expert in"—were phrases we used when an author was, in fact, green as a willow. And "endorsed by leaders in his field" we employed, also when reaching for straws, to explain that, if needed, a few of the author's friends might testify on their behalf.

There is only one instance of compulsively readable I know to have been true and I believe it because one of my professors was the teacher's assistant of David F. Swenson at the University of Minnesota, who told him about it, and from Swenson to my professor's ear to my own, seems a trustworthy chain. The book was Søren Kierkegaard's *Concluding Unscientific Postscript*, an unlikely tome for many of us to stay up all night reading; but Swenson did so, unable to put it down. He found it by chance on the shelves of the Minneapolis Public Library in 1901, in Danish. "[It] seemed to have a philosophical content," he said, "since a hasty turning of its leaves showed me that its pages were liberally sprinkled with abstruse philosophical terms." How fabulous it is that one could have found a thick philosophical work in a Scandinavian language in the public library stacks in Minneapolis in the early years of the twentieth century.

"The name of the author told me nothing," Swenson explained. He'd never heard of Kierkegaard. No one in North America had, then—expect perhaps the librarian who imported that rare book from Copenhagen to meet the needs of philosophically-inclined Danes recently immigrated to the Twin Cities. This was decades before Kierkegaardia ever saw English. Swenson was so moved that he did not sleep: "On a venture, I took the book home. It was Saturday evening, and I did not rise from the reading begun on reaching home, until half past two Sunday morning. By Sunday night I had finished the more than five hundred closely printed pages of the book, so impossible was it for me to lay it aside until I had finished it." Then he devoted the rest of his life to understanding the Danish writer, earning a PhD in philosophy, and teaching it at the University of Minnesota, as well as translating Kierkegaard into English.

The professor of mine who was Swenson's assistant was Paul L. Holmer. I became what some might call a "disciple" of his for three years, toward the end of his life. Retired from Yale, where he taught in both the University philosophy department and the Divinity School, Holmer returned to his Swedish Pietist roots for a month each year to teach the December term at our little North Park Theological Seminary in Chicago. I was in my early twenties, fresh out of college, and Holmer's Socratic style and religious piety appealed strongly to me. After taking his seminars on Wittgenstein/Kierkegaard (he wove them together) and C.S. Lewis, I promptly informed my supervisor I wanted to switch from the MDiv to the MA program and write my thesis on Holmer. So perhaps he is the reason why no one ever had to endure me as their pastor.

In 1990 and 1991 I published two essays about Holmer in a tiny journal out of Minnesota called *Pietisten*—printed on thick 11" x 17" textured paper, which was folded once and then stapled along the fold, to create a publication that looked like a menu in a good restaurant. One article was titled "Something about Holmer," an homage to him as well as to his old professor and friend, Swenson, who published one of the first books in English about Kierkegaard, calling it *Something about Kierkegaard* (1941). Today, that essay, and the other, read as more hero-worship than scholarship, but I'm still proud of them. Before leaving seminary to work in books, I saw the look of gratitude in Holmer's eyes one day at lunch when he encouraged me to enter a PhD program and teach in a university. "It's a wonderful way to spend a life," he wistfully said over his soup. But that wasn't the path for me.

I tell that story about Swenson's compulsive reading in part because Kierkegaard wrote in his journal three years after his *Concluding Unscientific Postscript* first appeared, that only about fifty copies had sold. Five zero. It had gone nowhere, fell flat, made no impression whatsoever. Yet, a copy somehow made its way to Minneapolis where Swenson found it on a shelf, and then stayed up all night reading it. That's magic, kismet, serendipity, and coalescence.

I have similar stories, and I imagine you do too. Books have an uncanny presence in our lives that goes unnoticed. Ralph Waldo Emerson once wrote to a friend, "It happens to us once or twice in a lifetime to be drunk with some book which probably has some extraordinary relative power to intoxicate us and none other." I would only change the word "intoxicate" to something more like "carry." And I have been blessed with this more than once or twice. I'd say, seventeen times so far.

Have you carried a book in your bag long after the time of reading it has passed, because it has become essential for you in ways that would be difficult to explain? Have you been caught holding a book close to your face, to better examine its paper or type, or even, to take in its smell? I recall the American interfaith teacher, Lex Hixon, commenting how in the 1960s his copy of *The Gospel of Sri Ramakrishna* smelled sweetly of fragrance only to discover a decade later that all of the copies of it were stored, before being sold, in the incense room at the Ramakrishna-Vivekananda Center on 94th Street in New York City. Several books in my life have held a metaphorical fragrance, and without the rational explanation.

So these are the books I have carried. I write for those who know that the hold books can have upon us can be difficult to explain, and the books we carry often say more about us than our clothes, our homes, even our spouses and children. I begin with a story from mid-life, only because it was in mid-life when I first began to realize the magic of books. Each chapter then builds onto the next, as I tell of books I've carried at pivotal moments, and those that have carried me from one place to another. You will experience a book that makes sense of a divorce and points the way to a new partner. A book opening up a subcontinent, and a gift for wonder. And how a book given to a young reader is able to carry him across a country to a bigger world. You will glimpse how a book stands in like a wise elder, when that is what is most of all needed, and a book that carried me like a raft across a rushing stream.

These stories are intimate, revealing, and confessional. Through them, I hope you will see more clearly your own stories of a life with books, your own particular "portable magic," to use Stephen King's knowing phrase, of how a volume can spark an understanding that comes before knowledge. While this memoir is personal, the essays are I hope universal in application for all readers and lovers of books. They show how the books we carry are more important than the food we eat.

CHAPTER 1

THE MARTIN BUBER BOOK I CARRIED
WHILE MY MARRIAGE FAILED

OOKS HAVE STORIES, and not only those told between their covers by their authors, or their publishers with marketing copy, but by readers who enjoy them. For me, *Tales of the Hasidim* by Martin Buber is a story that involves a failing marriage, an employer who I wanted to impress, the loneliness of business travel, and the associations that make a physical book unique.

I married in 1989, at twenty-one, much too early. From the start it was not a success. We had just completed college and I think we each felt compelled almost as part of the graduation ritual to pick a mate. I can still remember, after the honeymoon in London, Oxford, and Hay-on-Wye (the original "book town" in Wales), sitting one evening back in our Chicagoland apartment, looking at my young bride asleep and thinking, *What have I done?*

Two wonderful children came early, for which I will always be grateful. But neither husband nor wife were happy for long. We were unsuited for each other. Our disconnections far outweighed our connections. There was no wedded bliss.

Which is why, when, four years in, I had a job in publishing that required a lot of travel, that felt just fine. I was often gone week after week, Mondays through Fridays. After two years of that, I was promoted to a position with an even larger travel budget and expectation, with a boss who wanted me out of the office again with regular frequency. I was young and earnest and told to grow our business by finding new and unusual retail customers for our books. I did so with relish.

While sitting in marketing and editorial meetings in our downtown Minneapolis offices, I would jot on notepads the cities I might visit and names of retailers I might woo while there. This was the 1990s when brick and mortar retail was at its zenith. Barnes and Noble and Borders were wrestling each other for the most favorable spots on city blocks, and signing long-term leases. Department stores were regrowing book departments that they had diminished after initial experiments in the 1950s. Even Starbucks was selling books. It seemed that every serious retailer wanted a piece of the books business, not because books were very profitable, but because their presence seemed to raise the profile of customers who would walk through the doors.

The only reason I was ever in Walnut Creek, California to stumble upon my *Tales of the Hasidim* was because I had targeted a new toy company to try and convince them to stock our illustrated children's books. An early flight from Minneapolis/St. Paul to San Francisco, followed by a rental car counter and drive, lunch with a regular customer in Berkeley, and then a short drive to Walnut Creek, landed me in an enormous field of asphalt: the new toy company's parking lot.

The business appointment went quickly, as they always did. I never went in for the top-handed shake or dog and pony show presentations. Don't waste their time was my motto, and it seemed to work. I don't remember precisely but she may have been one of the potential customers with whom I obtained an appointment by assuring on the telephone, "I will be in and out of your office in less than ten minutes, I promise." This was said in response to, "I'm very busy. Just send me something in the mail and I'll look at it."

I *was* in and out that quickly. All the more amazing, remembering it now, is that I flew 2,000 miles on such a whim and a chance. Such were those optimistic days of seeking opportunities in the books biz.

So I then had a free afternoon and knew where I would go: to what I'd heard were the best used bookstores in the area. Top of that list was Bonanza Street Books, named the "Best of the East Bay," a store which is now sadly gone. It was the kind of used and out-of-print specialist that people on Yelp today complain about as "too stuffed with books," as if having difficulty moving about in a bookstore due to inventory excess were a negative thing.

Right away I saw the Buber on display in an area marked "New Arrivals." I picked it up and turned it over, probably in a way similar to how bread makers examine the bake of a loaf just out of the oven. I have seen a baker tap the bottom of a sourdough with his thumb, brush a forefinger across the top of the loaf, and then breathe in its aroma.

That author photo! I would have purchased this one for that alone. Then I opened the book to the middle and bent over slightly, to smell the pages. I cannot really explain this.

I knew the author and I knew of the book. I had read Buber's *I & Thou*, the book that everyone really knew him for, and felt that it changed my way of relating to other people and to God. Or at least it expanded my horizons a great deal. I had heard of the Hasidic tales and had read some of them from paperback volumes while standing in a library. But I had never seen the hardcover, and I frequented secondhand bookstores enough to know that it was scarce, especially in the dust jacket. So I snapped it up and didn't let it off my body until leaving an hour later. (As you look at other books, you tuck the treasured one in your armpit, so as to have free hands.)

There were two other aspects about the object that drew me to it that day. The first was a name stamped on the tail end of the book block: "Gordon L. Foster." I did not know who he was, alive or dead, but I suspected he was a book reviewer. More on that in a moment.

Tail end of a book block, stamped with the owner's name.

The second thing that appealed to me was tucked inside the front cover: a publisher's slip of paper sent with the book as a review copy. This reveals the publication date for *Tales of the Hasidim* as March 14, 1947. Mr. Foster must have valued his copy as evidenced by the stamping on the tail end, but also because he wrote his signature on the front flyleaf: "Gordon L. Foster," and underneath it, "New York 1946." This is how I knew he must have been a book reviewer, because he had the book in his hands at least three months before publication.

Many reviewers have been known to sell their unneeded copies to used book dealers, for cash. (I confess, I have done so.) But Mr. Foster's copy did not end up on a sale table at The Strand in Manhattan. At some point, it must have been packed into a box with the rest of his belongings for a move to the Bay Area, where I might find it half a century later. Just a bit of research while writing this chapter revealed that Gordon L. Foster at some point became a Protestant minister, serving churches in San Rafael and Mill Valley between 1950 and at least 1960—during which time I found evidence in the local newspapers of weddings and religious services he conducted.

Still, I have not addressed the meaning that this book held for me, then, and holds for me still. Only a book lover will understand when I say: I placed it in my shoulder bag—the bag that I carried with me everywhere every day—and it remained there for two years. I probably purchased or otherwise acquired two or three books a week during that time, but none displaced the position of this one in my bag.

Then I read it like a talisman, for the meaning of life. I cannot explain this fully either. I am sure that part of the appeal was the strangeness of the stories and the teachings in it. My life has had very little to correspond with the experiences of Lithuanian and Ukrainian Jews in the eighteenth century. Still, I immediately felt certain similarities between Hasidic teachings and tales and the teachings and tales of the Desert Fathers and Mothers of the early Christian tradition. These two from page 107 offer a good example:

> *To Say Torah and to Be Torah*
> Rabbi Leib, son of Sarah, the hidden zaddik [righteous man] who wandered over the earth, following the course of rivers, in order to redeem the souls of the living and the dead, said this: "I did not go to the maggid [preacher] in order to hear Torah from him, but to see how he unlaces his felt shoes and laces them up again."

> *How to Say Torah*
> The maggid once said to his disciples: "I shall teach you the best way to say Torah. You must cease to be aware of yourselves. You must be nothing but an ear which hears what the universe of the word is constantly saying within you. The moment you start hearing what you yourself are saying, you must stop."

Many of the tales highlight teachings of the Baal Shem Tov, the founder of Hasidic Judaism. In years to come I would spend hundreds of hours driving my car, and in rental cars on those frequent book-related trips, listening to two cassette tapes I purchased featuring the dramatic reading of the legends of the Baal Shem Tov by Austrian-American actor Theodore Bikel. His sonorous voice lent even more gravity to already redolent tales. I listened to the Hasidic masters through the lens of Martin Buber's tellings, and in the voice of Bikel's performances, both while riding in the Great Smoky Mountains, and lost on the winding streets of Boston.

But five years in, when the spell of the book began to wear off slightly, mostly because of overcrowding, and I at least was willing to release it from my shoulder bag, I discovered there was a second volume, also in hardcover. By that time, the internet was such that it was possible to find this other book without scouring bookstores, and I did so. This is of course the change that now goes unspoken, for those of us old enough to remember hunting for books before the internet. Many people back then carried handwritten lists in their wallets or purses of titles and authors to search for, whenever a bookstore appeared and they had a few minutes to spare. But *Tales of the Hasidim* did not have the same hold on me in its second volume.

It would be another decade before my unhappy marriage would end. When I first found my Buber I was somewhat numb. As A.N. Wilson, one of my favorite contemporary writers, recently explained his own experience in an unhappy early marriage, "My mind/soul, whatever you call it, was unable to recognize my marital sadness. I simply refused to articulate any such thoughts. Bottling it all up..." Yes. Except that I made lists, quietly during staff meetings, of where I might travel away from home, and on those journeys I searched and found books. And this one from Buber somehow helped to save me.

During that half decade of carrying *Tales of the Hasidim*, I left my job in Minneapolis and we moved to Vermont, where I went to work for seven years at a funky Jewish publishing house striving to create a transformative and spiritual list of books inspired by Judaism. We cultivated fresh and unique perspectives and styled ourselves "the Ben & Jerry's of spirituality publishing." Perhaps my Buber helped me in those transitions. I like to think it did. Because a goyish Christian guy heading up a marketing department for a Jewish book publisher always seemed odd to some, even if not to me. Did my Buber volume somehow carry me across that threshold?

I was exposed to more of Buber's work, then, as well as to Hasidic prayer, as we published some of the other great Hasidic masters, such as Rebbe Nachman of Breslov, who had an appeal beyond the Jewish community. It was my work to communicate these works to non-Jews like me. There was also the period of weeks, about five years after I began work with the Jewish press in Vermont, when I began to correspond and speak by phone with Buber's old personal friend and biographer, Maurice S. Friedman, who was in his eighties by then. Surprisingly, he was having trouble getting into print, even to publish a memoir about his work with Buber. I wanted to take him on, and help, but was unable to do so. Even then, the markets for books were beginning to shrink and those halcyon days were fading. Friedman died in 2012 and his obit appeared in the *New York Times*.

After seven years at the Jewish publishing house in Vermont, and two years after the end of my first marriage, working now back on the Christian side of book publishing, I met the new rabbi in our small Vermont town. We didn't talk about Martin Buber, but I suspect Buber had something to do with introducing us. I asked if she would like to get a glass of wine. She didn't much like me at first, but said yes. Within six months we were engaged. We are still married, and I am still a goyish Christian guy learning from Jews and Judaism. I now know that Martin Buber is credited as one of the founders of what is called neo-Hasidism—a revival of Hasidic spirituality in the wake of modernism's assault on the original Hasidic movement in Eastern Europe—precisely because Buber wrote and published his work on the Hasidic masters in German for an audience that was as much Christian as it was Jewish.

The reason why that second volume of Buber's Hasidic tales did not fill me with as much curiosity and passion as the first one did, will remain a mystery. Perhaps the old adage is true: When the student is ready, the teacher will appear. My teacher was Buber (and then some), but even more importantly, and certainly more magical and inexplicably, was the importance of that particular volume I carried. That singular copy. My best explanation for the thrill, the "magic," is really no explanation at all: certain books, for complicated and varied reasons, enchant us and in ways that are not easily duplicated.

CHAPTER 2

THREE INCHES OF HITLER
IN VERY SMALL HANDS

HE FACT THAT my parents thought it was odd, and my teacher found it upsetting, made my possession of John Toland's giant paperback about Adolf Hitler all the more pleasing. I purchased it at the only bookstore I knew at the time: a Crown Books in the strip mall where my parents bought our groceries. Crown sold mostly bestsellers, and this one was on the *New York Times* list. "The Titanic Bestseller!" it proclaimed in a burst at the top of the front cover, followed by "6 Months on the New York Times List!" It was also, at 1,400 pages, plus thirty-two thicker inset pages of photographs, one of the fattest mass market paperbacks ever produced when it appeared in September 1977.

This chapter is about a child's desire to be taken seriously, the sometimes rough and sudden transition from childhood to adulthood, and the ways that we are drawn to what is outside and beyond our direct experience. I suppose it should also be about my heroic parents who let my odd book interests grow without interference. They saw me carrying it. They trusted me, unlike so many parents before and since, to be able to handle painful knowledge of the world.

It was when I was about nine that I stopped walking the aisles of the grocery store with mom and dad. The child who'd hung on the grocery cart, anxious to select his own breakfast cereal and open freezer doors to choose tater tots and ice creams, was suddenly disinterested in all that. So I sat instead on the lower shelf of the magazines display, leafing through copies of *Teen Beat*. I remember the cover photographs and pull-out pin-ups of stars like Donny and Marie Osmond, of course David and Shaun Cassidy, and for a time I took to parting my hair down the middle in a fruitless attempt at imitating those dreamboats. After about a year of this malingering in the grocery store magazine aisle (I'm surprised, now, that it took so long), this too grew stale, and so at ten years old I discovered the existence of Crown in the same strip mall, and asked mom if I might spend the hour there. It was only a few stores away. This is where I had my first bookstore browsing experiences.

I suppose there were children growing up in Manhattan in the 1970s who remember exploring The Strand before they ever read George Eliot or could pronounce Kierkegaard, and there were kids raised in the Twin Cities or downtown Chicago or Milwaukee who discovered subjects such as Feminist Studies, Religion, and Books on Books by browsing in the wonderful local independent bookstores in those places. But for me, growing up in the burbs, Crown was my one and everything at the start. I'd seen a B. Dalton, too, in our shopping mall, but my family rarely stopped there. I walked into Crown on that first occasion and thought, *Every book one might want, is here.* It would be a few years before I knew how wrong that was. Never mind. It was, at ten, universe-expanding.

I picked up *Adolf Hitler* out of curiosity and a sense of horror. I'd heard the name and knew that evil was associated with it, and wondered if it was acceptable to write and read about such terrible things. A child is taught not to look at what is horrifying, and to stay away from what is dangerous. Huge type on the first page proclaimed, "John Toland Has Given the Demon a Human Face."

I was soon to enter the sixth grade. I had the $2.95 required in my pocket—newspaper delivery money—and that was a bargain.

The currency equivalent today is about fifteen dollars, but you would never find a book such as this today for less than twenty-five. Publishers made books cheaper then, believing they would lure consumers of magazines and candy bars into readers of books. I think I was headed for the books anyway, but it helped to find serious ones near the comic books and M&Ms.

It was 2 ¼ inches thick when I brought it home from the store, but expanded to more than that, as I began to read.

The author John Toland was an interesting character who wrote a Pulitzer Prize winner before he wrote about Hitler, and failed at being a playwright and short story writer before both of those. But this is not a story about John Toland, interesting as he may have been. This is also not a story about the content of my fat Hitler paperback. It was a thorough presentation of the rise and fall of one of the twentieth century's most despicable people; it was devastating to read, especially for a child, and opened my eyes to a world where mass murder and diabolic activity is not only possible but common. John Toland's actual sentences did not matter. I remember none of them now. The paperback sits on my shelf today because I purchased another copy forty years after first reading it, feeling wistful for my loss of ignorance.

I didn't know it then, but I was practicing reading as a virtue. There's nothing wrong with this. In fact, I suspect that a good percentage of the books on people's shelves right now are symbols of intention more than they are representations of actual reading experiences. I also imagine there were would-be intellectuals hitching scrolls to their girdles two centuries before Christ, in Athens, to distinguish themselves from those chasing chariots and throwing javelins. When Rome was falling, in fifth-century Europe, there were surely people carrying codices under their arms—intent on being seen doing so —to signal membership in a particular school of thought. Even on the North American continent, could it be that Indigenous people had, if not readers, but storytellers who told their tales not simply because it was their gift to do so but because by doing so it meant they were not doing something else?

This sort of book carrying continued in me for a long time. A couple years after I carried John Toland's *Adolf Hitler*, after a visit to see family in Oregon, and a few extended conversations with my retired pastor-grandfather, whom I adored, I returned home and used paper route money to mail-order six-volumes of the sermons of the nineteenth-century English Baptist preacher, Charles Spurgeon. I did this not so much to impress my Baptist Grandpa, because he lived 2,000 miles away, but with the idea that reading those sermons would make me more like him. I did read them daily, underlining passages with a ruler-guided pencil here and there. I wasn't exactly virtue-signaling. But long after the daily reading ended—and that was probably about three weeks in—I felt, in some indescribable ways that possessing those books was essential to my identity. Until my identity changed, which of course it did. So, in a way, this is a story about how books can be critically important to us even when their contents have only a generic impact on our hearts and minds.

It is also worth mentioning how habits tend to last: I lie to people all the time, now, forty-plus years later, as I am asked, "What are you reading now?" because I never admit that I'm still sometimes reading books of sermons. Not Spurgeon, not since childhood. But today I still turn to the sermons, homilies, *derasha*, and dharma talks of the ordained and otherwise religiously committed to opening the hidden meaning in scriptures, and helping point people on their spiritual paths. Just recently I attended Friday prayers with a young Muslim friend and afterwards we spent ninety minutes discussing the sermon over pizza. I grew up believing that there is power intrinsic in those words—or at least there can be—and I've never lost that pull.

There is a story in my family from about this time in my life, when Toland's *Adolf Hitler* was in my hands, that my desire to become a writer first surfaced. After what must have been a particularly stimulating science class at school, I settled one afternoon into an overstuffed living room chair in the home of my piano teacher. My older brother and I took lessons each week on the same afternoon, and I would sit and wait during his lesson, until it was my turn, in one of those chairs. With a spiral notebook and a pen, I headed the top of the first page, "The Liver, by Jon Sweeney." I was determined to write a complete treatise on the subject, and used my best cursive to longhand all my thoughts and research up to that point. I must have written furiously for about five minutes. I think I filled a quarter of one page. That was all I had. This was virtue reading turning to virtue writing. Many years later, when he knew I was writing a real book, my father one afternoon said casually on the phone, "How is that book on the liver coming along?"

I was motivated to carry *Adolf Hitler* because I wanted to be more than a simple boy. And, like any child, the pictures helped. I close my eyes today and can recite for you the photographs reproduced in the insert section, so often did I stare at them. There was the one of "Baby Adolf." *He could be me.* And below it, the baby's very forbidding looking father. Two pages later and there were three photos of Adolf ages ten, eleven, and twelve, among his schoolmates. *He looks just like boys I know at school, and want to avoid at all costs.*

A century ago, Russian philosopher Nicolas Berdyaev hit the nail on the head when he observed, "The pursuit of knowledge is undoubtedly one of the ways of overcoming solitude; it compels us to abandon our self-centred isolation, and situates us in another space and time where we are brought in contact with the Other Self. It is an escape from solitude, a way of getting to know the other Ego, the divine world." This is beyond the joy of reading, and also beyond reading for information, which means it is an understanding of a life with books that is outside of the experiences of most human beings, and mostly impossible to communicate.

There is no escaping the pain and suffering of the world, Toland's *Adolf Hitler* taught me that at a young age. Perhaps too young. But the effect it had on an elementary school child is probably no different from what my daughter has experienced studying the Holocaust in school, or hearing gunshots at night in our Milwaukee neighborhood. Still, both then and now, I could never follow Iris Murdoch, in all those Buddhist moments in her novels (I read a lot of them), where she says, "The world is perhaps ultimately to be defined as a place of suffering," a place of "ceaseless anxiety and pain and fear…. That this world is a place of *horror* must affect every serious artist and thinker."

I'm not sure. I wouldn't ultimately trade any of the experiences with books I have carried. Trying to explain the power that a book has had upon you, for good, is sometimes like trying to articulate what it was like to veer off a bridge in a car, become trapped inside of it underwater, and then find your way back to the surface, gasping for air, filled with something that is more than gratitude can express.

CHAPTER 3

A MEANS OF ESCAPE
WITH *MY SIDE OF THE MOUNTAIN*

HERE HAVE BEEN many happy moments in my life that did not involve books, but I rarely remember them. Joyful times often pass like clouds on a pleasant summer afternoon, but *bookhood*—a "book's physical autonomy and life-ish-ness"—leaves a mark. Emma Smith coins that term in her lovely *Portable Magic*. A book's bookhood is its unique qualities that allow it to grab hold of us.

I'm not sure if Smith means this, but I do: no two copies of a book are the same.

The French philosopher who died in 2021, Jean-Luc Nancy, used different language to express this idea. He said that every book is "sacred" in that it "poses and imposes itself at one and the same time as a given, fully formed, integral and nonmodifiable entity, while also opening itself liberally to reading, which will never stop opening it wider and deeper, giving it a thousand sense or a thousand secrets, rewriting it, finally, in a thousand ways."

Then he added that every book is an "imprint" in that "The engraved and impressed characters now repeated in numerous copies on mobile supports, like those that preceded them, traced with a stylus and copied numerous times on skin, bark, or silk, comprise the imprint, the impregnation and pregnancy that the book is big and heavy with, whose volume, in fact, is nothing other than its womb and gravidity."

I'm not sure if Jean-Luc Nancy means this, but I do: that particular volume, no matter its subject, in its qualities as a sacred, imprinted thing, can be like a womb.

This is a story about that bookish womb, in childhood, learning to love spending time alone, and how a book can help express our worries and fears. Before we really know how to feel, the language of a book helps to give our feelings voice. I wouldn't suggest that this happens all the time. In fact, if we're fortunate, there will be just a few books in our lives possessing bookhood in a way that latches on, and when they do, it is clear—back to Emma Smith wisdom— that "form matters" and "we read form almost unconsciously as an aggregate of the senses before, and alongside, reading the words on the page."

My copy of Jean Craighead George's *My Side of the Mountain* had wrinkled waffle-patterned pages characteristic of a book that's been left out in a light rain. Some earlier young reader had done so, before returning the book to the school library where I found it. I was in seventh grade.

There are books we read, and then there are those that we dream with. This was a dreaming book. I was fearful, in all of the usual ways. Every child is afraid, whether or not they demonstrate it in front of you. We ponder frightening things that our parents prefer to pretend don't exist. Monsters under the bed are real possibilities. Death is the most obvious of these things that frighten. I remember attending my first funeral, for an old man I knew from church. It was an open-casket affair and for two nights after seeing him lying there I cried myself to sleep, not for him so much as in a sudden, painful realization that my parents would also someday be gone. I don't remember talking about this with either my mother or my father at the time, and I don't remember them noticing or hearing my crying at night. Or maybe they thought my crying was part of a process.

We also sometimes pretend in order to cope with what's otherwise impossible to face. This must be why so many children are drawn to play-fighting with pretend weapons, or more often today, violent games on their electronic devices and screens. When blood spurts in imaginative play, it allows us to cope with the fears we don't express about our real blood, which we hope never spurts.

For as long as I can remember, I have craved time alone. I spent a great deal of time in solitude as a child, usually by choice. So when I found *My Side of the Mountain*, it allowed an eleven-year-old boy to imagine running away from his suburban home to live with an owl in the woods, a delicious fantasy of self-reliance that I still seriously entertain. Although it began as a library book for me, and I carried it for so long that my mother ended up paying large fines. Then, for several years after I began reading *My Side of the Mountain*, I dreamed at night that Craighead George's character Sam was in fact me; that I too had run away from home; and that like Sam, I was living by my wits in the woods with birds and animals as my best friends.

It was that magical opening sentence. "I am on my mountain in a tree home that people have passed without ever knowing that I am here"—which speaks to every child's feeling at one time or another of being invisible, of not mattering, and yet knowing otherwise in their gut. It also brought a certain measure of comfort that I could stand on my own if necessary. Maybe, like Sam, I was all that I needed. Because kids know that their people will someday die. It was when I was five, and attended that first funeral, when I realized that everyone dies, and with that sudden bursting of my bubble, and after silently crying myself to sleep for two nights, I was no longer a little boy. On the third day, I got up and put away my sadness.

In the daylight, I would fantasize about the things I was reading in Sam's life. Even into young adult, married life, career, and travel to faraway places, I would imagine I was still all alone in the world with no one to look out for me. No one loving me. No one knowing me like my pet owl. Like Sam, I would feel that I too could, or would, leave everyone I knew behind in search of something else in the mountains.

In Craighead's novel, Sam narrates his leaving New York City one day in May with only "a penknife, a ball or cord, an ax, and $40 which I had saved from selling magazine subscriptions." I too had sold magazine subscriptions door-to-door; I also had a paper route—the old-fashioned kind, rolling papers on the living room floor, wrapping each with a rubber band, placing them in a cloth shoulder bag, and delivering them on my bicycle, throwing each one as hard as I could at the metal screen doors of my neighbors.

Sam makes preparations for leaving home, for becoming independent. In my version of Sam's fantasy, I pondered, *I have five dollars. How long can I make it last?* I knew I didn't need to purchase much. My fantasy quickly took on serious tones and I remember making many lists of necessities, planning as if for the inevitable and ordinary reality to come soon. I was dead serious, as if my apocalyptic future were likely to begin tomorrow. One list looked like this, and became my *My Side of the Mountain* bookmark:

> Gallon of milk, 95 cents
> Loaf of bread, 50 cents
> Bananas—six, 35 cents
> Red licorice, 25 cents
> $2.95 left over.

What can I say, I loved red candy.

My Side of the Mountain carried me into the woods, but here I use the word "woods" metaphorically, like a mystic recalling the place where mystics before him have met the Source of their

Mystery. "Wilderness" and "desert" are words that work equally as well. My woods were no less unknown to me than were Sam's, even though mine were in fact a large piece of Illinois prairie. I was a young reader in the late 1970s in the west suburbs of Chicago, in the fastest growing county in the United States, where some of the last family farms were being bought up by developers seeking to meet housing demands. One thirty-acre farm bordered the neighborhood where my parents built a new house for us when I was in second grade, and I watched as the prairie grasses and pheasants who lived in their depths, slowly ebbed away.

My Side of the Mountain took me and also allowed me to go to lonely places where we decide to face our aloneness. Only because of the companionship of this book was I able to begin to experience a contemplative life (contemplatives face their death honestly) as a child. I have never really left the places where it took me. The biblical David, who every kid like me reads about, watching him face adult realities while still young and small, would write of how "deep calls to deep" in the forty-second psalm, calling to mind the cave or hole in the tree in the woods where Sam finds his secret, safe meaning. Like David, I was also finding the living God in those places, both real and imaginary. Jacob, before him in the Bible, slept one night with a stone for a pillow. I could do that.

These feelings and this need for help with fear did not just go away when I became a teenager. In the suburbs of Chicago, in Wheaton, where I grew up, the Tylenol killer snuck potassium cyanide into painkilling medication, murdering seven people beginning in late September 1982. I was then fifteen. One man died in the Arlington Heights hospital, near the mall where my family shopped on weekends. One woman died in Winfield, the town next to ours, where we lived before my parents built that house near the prairie grasses. And a few weeks after that woman's death, as everyone wondered what next from the supermarket shelves would be poison-tainted, investigators found cyanide in the capsules of a Tylenol bottle purchased from a grocery in downtown Wheaton not far from our house.

Fast forward some thirty years, after carrying Craighead George's book around by myself, I had two reading-age children of my own and *My Side of the Mountain* found me again. I saw it looking back at me from the shelves of Commonwealth Books, when that secondhand shop was still on Boylston Street facing the Common. I was there at least once a month for many years, driving long distances, dragging my young children with me. We lived in a log cabin on twenty acres in the Vermont woods (me living like Sam) but my mind and spirit were often moving in the direction of Boston and New York (but not really). It sounded good, that we lived in a log cabin in the woods—my first authored books carried this information in the author bios on their dust jackets—but the truth was that I was much more Whitman than Thoreau, even if I idealized the latter most. Whitman wrote:

> Keep your splendid silent sun,
> Keep your woods O Nature, and the quiet places by the
> woods,
> Keep your fields of clover and timothy, and your corn-
> fields and orchards,
> … Give me faces and streets…
> Give me interminable eyes … give me comrades and
> lovers by the thousand!

I was frequently packing up the kids, who were more than willing, to drive to the city. Boston was a day trip. Two-and-a-half hours down, two-and-a-half hours back, with a couple bookstores, a ride on the T from Park Street to Harvard Square in Cambridge, lunch, and some play on Boston Common in between. That play also occasionally involved a thoughtful stroll through Central Burying Ground, the eighteenth-century cemetery near where Boylston

meets Tremont, amid ancient trees that easily turned my imagination back again to what it might be like to carve one out and live
alone inside it. With my owl.

CHAPTER 4

FORBIDDEN BOOKS FOR
ORDINARY TEENAGE TRAUMA

HERE'S A DISTINCT pleasure in the elicit book, the one that your parents told you never to open. This chapter is a pause to remember what I hope every reader has, at times, been able to do: carry a forbidden book in their pockets, or hide one under the mattress. This is also my recognition of the seeming randomness of how we discover what we read, how it then comes to define us, and how our finding of a book is just as likely, in fact, as that book finding us. Discovery, if we allow ourselves to be open to it, can be like following the strangest patterns of clues. What pleasure it can be! And nothing is sweeter than our youthful dalliances with things our elders warned us against.

The private Christian high school I attended was, thank God, resident to a couple of extraordinary teachers. Whether by subtle rebellion or simple cleverness, they were able to stimulate progressive attention to the world of emotion and ideas, regardless of the otherwise required creeds and compulsory chapel services. One of these teachers was my freshman year Bible instructor. Our class gathered daily for two semesters, working our way through the entirety of the Protestant Christian Bible, from Old Testament to New Testament, Genesis to Revelation. We would read, analyze, and discuss. Quizzes and tests measured our comprehension and memory.

One Friday in early winter, as we finished the twelfth and final chapter of the book of Ecclesiastes, and our instructor was concluding his lecture, the bell rang. As we all began to rapidly pack our things, to rush along to our next classes, the teacher called out, "Just a minute, everyone! Before you go." Most of us were standing, backpacks on shoulders. He said, "On Monday morning, we would normally move directly to the next book in the canon. However, in this one case, I don't think that it is an appropriate text for teenagers to read and discuss. So, we will move directly past the Song of Solomon, and on Monday we will begin the first of what are called the prophetic books: Isaiah."

The following Monday morning, with all our teenage bodies back in our seats in that classroom, the instructor walked to the front of the room and stood behind the lectern. He looked at us all slowly, with a grin, and we were looking back at him, a bit unsure of what was happening. He said, "So. What did y'all think of the Song of Solomon? Did you know it's also called the Song of Songs?"

Ah, "Let him kiss me with the kisses of his mouth!" Those were the days.

I would discover many years later, beginning with reading the medieval monastic, St. Bernard of Clairvaux, and then sitting in a class taught by one of his spiritual heirs, M. Basil Pennington, that Christian mystics spend days, even weeks, expounding on that first sentence, which is the opening verse of the Song of Songs. Pennington had trouble moving beyond it, he had so much to say.

Teachers of other religious traditions, too: Bhakti, in Hinduism, for instance, resonates with similar themes, of the intense emotional, devotional, and physical attachment between a personal God and a human being. What does it mean for a human being to so desire the kiss of God that it becomes something expressed in downright sexual terms? What might the "kisses of the mouth" be, in contrast to other kinds of kissing? And then, to be in one's bed, wishing for the one whom you desire most urgently? This is the language of that "forbidden" text, and there are many ways of imagining what it all means.

There is "My beloved is to me a bag of myrrh that lies between my breasts" (Song of Songs 1:13), and other such examples from the text, which the mystics have a bit tougher time wrapping into the metaphorical relationship between God and humankind. But they do so; mystics are nothing if not acrobatic.

There's no question that teenagers will have a ball with these passages—and it is absolutely necessary that they read and enjoy them. As a great psychologist said about fairytales in which frightened children push mean old people into ovens: kids need to read them, or have them read to them, not despite the violence and ugly emotions, but because of them, because children have such feelings (even the awful ones) and haven't yet figured out how to manage them.

Has there ever been a teenager who hasn't had sexual thoughts, a stir of curious and erotic imaginings? "Upon my bed at night I sought him whom my soul loves" (Song of Songs 3:1)—and they have no idea what to do with such curiosities. Left to themselves— to *ourselves*, because that enlightened teacher of mine was an outlier in such matters, and we were in fact *not* permitted to really discuss what we had read—who knows where the stirring will take them.

There was another day during my first year of high school when I was riding in the backseat of an upper classman's car. The radio was on and my elders were talking in the front seat, ignoring the kid in back, so a song caught my attention in a way it normally might not have. A nasally pierce of a voice was singing a melancholy ballad to the hard strumming of an acoustic guitar. Then I heard harmonica. This was all new to me. I knew nothing of folk music until this moment. Leaning back to the rear deck speaker behind my head, listening for the radio host to say the name of the artist, I heard "Bob Dylan" for the first time. A few days later, I used caddying money to buy his self-titled first album, the one with the boyish face in a hat on the cover. I listened to the record on the record player in my room, quiet enough to go unnoticed at home. A few weeks after that, I bought *The Times They Are A-Changin'* and soon I was singing "Spanish Boots of Spanish Leather" as if I knew the feelings of a spurned lover. Quickly on the heels of it came *Blood on the Tracks*, on which I heard Dylan sing the quick line, "Mine have been like Verlaine's and Rimbaud's" in the song "You Gonna Make Me Lonesome When You Go." He was referring to a string of failed relationships with women. I of course had no idea what any of it really meant, nor even how the line went, since it's sung so quickly in the song. And I knew French Symbolist poets about as much as I knew then—or now—quantum physics or the way to a woman's heart. Still, I kept following the threads like breadcrumbs in a forest.

A few days later, I went to the public library and approached the reference desk. "Is there someone named Ran-bo?" I hesitantly asked the reference librarian. This was precisely when Sylvester Stallone had incarnated a fictional bloodthirsty character called Rambo in the first film of that franchise. In fact, John Rambo first appeared in David Morrel's crackerjack thriller, *First Blood*, which was then made into a crackerjack movie of the same name. The librarian looked at me patronizingly. "*Ram*-bo?" "No," I said. "Where did you read this name?" she asked. "I didn't," I said, "I heard it in a Bob Dylan song." "Oh, which one?" she said; I'd lucked upon a Dylan fan. So I ran through the lyrics before the line, and then the line itself. "I think *Rimbaud* is who you are looking for," the librarian concluded. Then it turned out our library shelved nothing by the French poet.

Weeks went by, perhaps months, those early teenage years are a messy memory. Sometime later I was in the tiny, and only, secondhand bookshop in my town and spied a battered black-and-white paperback with the name Rimbaud on the spine. *A Season in Hell and The Drunken Boat*, published by New Directions. (This would lead me into the thickets of James Laughlin's publishing house, the birth of modernism and imagism, Ezra Pound, William Carlos Williams, Denise Levertov, and other riches, but none of those did I carry around like a talisman as I did Arthur Rimbaud at the age of fourteen.)

Discovery is tender in our teenage years. Everything is tender, then, and these are matters that touch both body and soul. At precisely the time I was first arriving at "formed religious convictions," to use Cardinal Newman's phrase, I was also having my dalliance with forbidden books. Arthur Rimbaud embodied my rebellion, which was more bookish than real. I think this is why I came out the other end a religious progressive rather than something...*more daring*. By some alchemy I blended religious practice with agnostic doubt into something that makes sense at least in the secret of my own heart and imagination.

I arrived in high school after the dreaded junior high, which I'm convinced left most of us suffering from PTSD. In junior high, there were daily fistfights in the parking lot, regulated fear in the hallways. These experiences are universal, I gather, from reading novels and the memoirs of others, and mine were no different. What more can be expected when a few hundred eleven to thirteen-year-olds, brimming with curiosity, steaming with hormones, and experimenting with freedom, are placed together between four walls every day all day? It was junior high where I learned why and how to carry my books and papers from class to class nervously high in the crook of an elbow, never down low casually at my side. If you carried too low, without at least a bicep wrapped around them, some idiot would sneak from behind and flick them out of your hand to the floor. Then a small crowd of he and his cronies, plus pathetic others who'd already learned this lesson the hard way, would stare and laugh as you sprawled about to gather your things once again.

My other defense, developed like a mammal in the wild under constant threat, was to learn a mouth of obscenities like a boxer does punches. I spoke with language at school that my parents would not have recognized. Arriving home at the end of a day, for the first few weeks, I would shudder, contemplating the day's blasphemies, irreverences, and crudities; but then, a few weeks in, it became so commonplace that it no longer felt like something for which to beg forgiveness. It was survival behavior. My brother, two years older, had gone through similar junior high trauma and so decided to plead with our parents to attend the private Christian high school two towns over instead of matriculating to the very large public high school nearby where most of the creeps were headed.

I remember the conversation at the dinner table. No one in our family had ever considered a private school education. We weren't private school people, but these were desperate times. My clever mother responded, a few weeks later, by applying for a job as executive secretary to the headmaster of the private school, making my brother's tuition there gratis, and mine, too, two years later. I don't regret attending there—although the higher moral code proved elusive, especially on the afternoon during freshman year when three football players met me in an empty hallway and decided it would be fun to "pants" me, which means forcibly remove my blue jeans. There must be loads of literature on what it means, and how it happens, that a young person makes it through the confusion of teenage years with a self-image and religious identity still intact. Permanent fractures must be more common than reconfigured wholes.

However, the discontinuity from eighth grade to ninth—from chaos to something relatively peaceful—did rattle my soul. Most of my new schoolmates had matriculated from a private school for grades K-8, to this Christian high school. The quietude of the new situation felt disingenuous to what I knew of the world by this time, and even if Rimbaud was an overreach, he helped. He was part of my quiet rebellion—of words, privately enjoyed—a dalliance with the dangerous and forbidden that is held in the custody of the eyes through silent reading. And the path that started with a Bob Dylan song also stuck to me, since I realized that, like Dylan (Robert Zimmerman, raised in little Hibbing, Minnesota), I didn't have to remain who I was then, but could become who I wanted to be.

I discovered that Rimbaud recreated himself, too, writing fast and furiously, maturing quickly into something unlike what he'd been originally poised to become. He set out recreating, and did so thoroughly before the age of twenty. All his poetry was written between the ages of seventeen and nineteen. And—I learned much later—he walked very fast wherever he went. His friend Paul Verlaine (from the Dylan song) nicknamed him, "the man with soles of wind," because Verlaine had such a difficult time keeping up with Rimbaud walking around Paris.

I too started to walk fast. Being bookish did not have to be sedentary. The Leonard Bast character in *Howard's End* talks of walking through the night, all night, one Saturday into Sunday morning, reading *The Ordeal of Richard Feverel*, imitating its hero who does the same. I'd also read of the days-long and weeks-long trekking of writers like William Wordsworth and Samuel Taylor Coleridge and I wanted to emulate them, but was usually too tethered to my domestic situations to do so. I could not—have never been able to—remove myself from that basic posture of obedience in which I was brought up.

Young Rimbaud's phrases about strangling joy, purging his mind of hope, arming himself against justice, and cursing beauty were like an antidote to the saccharine sureties of my childhood faith that needed to be strangled. The poet helped me do that once and for all.

But in *The Drunken Boat*, Rimbaud speaks of wanting to sink into the sea, and I wasn't about to follow him there. I saw through the pessimism, and how he was also filled with more than rebellion. Even his darkness was infused with something holy and seeking for possibility. The seeking for something else, was in itself, spiritual and meaningful.

As I carried that black-and-white paperback in my high school backpack, all of Rimbaud's wanderings into the erotic and rebellious were not imitated by me so much as they were carefully observed and tabled. I wasn't supposed to be pondering seasons in hell or drunken boats with a dead French poet, and yet I was doing that—in the bleachers and at pep rallies. It was a thin book, easily thumbed, and fit neatly inside a school folder.

Rimbaud's biographers tell us he spent decades in obscurity, when his teenage creativity was gone, many of those years in Africa completely lost to history, and writing nothing. Many people have searched for missing manuscripts, convinced that the quick-learning spirit-fed teenage poet must have kept on with his pen. But nothing has been found. He left his friends behind too, as well as his rebellions, apparently, since there was news of a deathbed confession and return to his Catholic faith in the summer of 1891. I never really left in a way that made it necessary to dramatically return, but only because Arthur did it for me.

CHAPTER 5

IN SEARCH OF WENDELL BERRY
AND A LIFE WITHOUT EXPECTATIONS

FELL IN with Wendell Berry early. At sixteen, believing that there must be a bookstore with more to offer than the Crown Books in our grocery store strip mall, and with a fresh driver's license, I made my way to an independent on the Fox River in Chicago's west suburbs a few miles past my high school. Early that summer, I spent my first afternoon there, and left too much of the money I'd been earning working on weekends. Then I returned again and again. The booksellers would allow me to linger with vagrancy for hours: sitting to read, taking notes, asking questions.

A real bookstore was new to me, a good one like a discovered foreign land. I don't remember my parents ever taking me to a bookstore. We were, I suppose, more of a library card family. Finding this place happened while eating ice cream with a friend at the creamery next door. It was the next day, after school, with a borrowed car, that I made my way back to look at books. All the better, the serendipity, because what we find on our own always becomes the sweetest of discoveries. But this is not a story about ice cream and bookstores, so much as it is about seeing the smallnesses of life, living accidentally with purpose, and accepting with gratitude that the path we take is rarely planned, linear, or certain.

The bookseller who owned my new favorite place was a smart and indulgent woman. I felt welcomed to hang around and ask questions, and I had many. She observed my interests and soon was remembering my patterns, suggesting books. She even seemed to know what I wasn't saying. "Stay as long as you like," I remember from one afternoon, followed by, "You don't always have to buy something."

It happened then, after several weeks of impromptu conversations, that we realized together how I was on the weekends caddying for her husband at a private golf club. "I'm Mary Lou Kelly," she announced, and then asked where I was from. She remarked how I seemed to spend more money on books than other teenagers she knew. "I caddy all summer," I said. "Where do you do that?" she asked. "Chicago Golf Club." "Well, then you might know my husband." "Of course," I said, "Mr. Kelly."

Mary Lou became my first literary friend, and she was twenty years older than my parents. My tastes were rapidly evolving from the religious and Christian into something much wider, including modern literature, ecology, poetry, and philosophy. I soon learned that there were implicitly religious people who wrote explicitly about these wider matters. No one had told me that before.

One day, Mary Lou put two books by a Kentucky farmer, Wendell Berry, in my hands: *The Wheel*, a little book of poems, and *Recollected Essays*. "I think you will like him," she said, setting them down beside me, then walking briskly away.

I noticed their physical uniqueness: they were paperbacks with French flaps. I didn't know the phrase "French flaps" then; I just thought they were cool. Berry's long-time publisher was Jack Shoemaker, and in the 1970s and '80s Shoemaker was running North Point Press from San Francisco, and his press became known for using the French flap paperback on poetry, novels, and literary essays, and for publishing some of the most interesting writers of the late twentieth century including M.F.K. Fisher, Jean Giono,

Guy Davenport, and Hugh Kenner. And a young Wendell Berry. But I digress—Mary Lou…she said, wandering by about five minutes later, "You should get to know Wendell Berry." And that's all she said, before returning to the cash register to answer someone else's questions. She knew how true discoveries work best. It had to be my own.

I sat and read, and read. I bought *The Wheel* that day—probably because it was new, had been published that year, 1984—but also because of the way the poems were typeset on the page. I didn't yet know about poetry design, fonts, and white space, but those things compelled my young eyes in their own way, like I imagine spoons work on the table of a tea ceremony. I came back with caddying money for *Recollected Essays* the following week, and when Mary Lou wasn't there, I almost didn't buy it. But I did buy it, and then returned a few days later to talk with her about it.

I read both books immediately and then over and over. Soon I was giving copies to friends, as if I had become the wise and experienced bookseller. And Wendell Berry became one of *those* authors in my life: He was walking a road that drew me, and articulating what the road was that I already sensed I was walking on.

My favorite essay from *Recollected Essays*, ever since that first reading, is the one called "An Entrance to the Woods." I am sure my loving it was because it was wisdom completely unknown to me, suburban teenager that I was. Except for the sense of loneliness it portrayed. I've never known a book hound or library cormorant who didn't understand what it was to be lonely, sometimes deliciously so. I wanted what "An Entrance to the Woods" wanted, and what it seemed also to possess.

The narrator—we have every reason to believe it is Berry himself—describes leaving his work in the city and driving east until reaching a watershed of the Red River in the Daniel Boone National Forest along the Cumberland Plateau in eastern Kentucky. From there, he turns on to a service road and follows that to a foot trail. It is clear that this is not the first time he has been to this place. He is in the habit of returning. Berry writes what comes next:

> It is nearly five o'clock when I start walking. The afternoon is brilliant and warm, absolutely still, not enough air stirring to move a leaf. There is only the steady somnolent trilling of insects, and now and again in the woods below me the cry of a pileated woodpecker. Those, and my footsteps on the path, are the only sounds.

That stillness, those sounds and nearly silent footsteps in wild places, were something I hadn't experienced firsthand, but they immediately made sense. In a decade when I also was discovering Rabindranath Tagore and Martin Buber, I believe it was Berry who first taught me to seek solitude, to find meaning in wild places, and the benefits of being still and quiet. These were not wild places that were somehow "pristine," as some other nature writers have portrayed land stolen from Indigenous people and supposedly discovered by Europeans. These were wild places with history—some of that history was unknown to the writer, some of it related to his own ancestors in those same places. Berry wrote in order to listen to where he was, where he was going, and where he had come from. I have not always followed his advice, but I think my life has been richer when I have.

A few years later, as a college sophomore, I explained to three friends who Wendell Berry was. They nodded disinterestedly. Then I added that I had access to a car for spring break and intended to drive to Kentucky to find him. This was suddenly an adventure worth tagging along. I still smile, remembering the four of us meandering the knobs of Kentucky on spring break as many of our friends headed to beaches with beer kegs.

This was a couple of decades before GPS and at least ten years before internet searches. I knew only two things: The blurbs on

Berry's book jackets referred to Port Royal, Kentucky as the place where he lived with his wife, and there was a woodcut illustration in one book that seemed to be an illustration of his home and farm. So we drove from Chicago south, following a map (remember maps?), to Louisville, Kentucky, and then made our way on smaller roads to the junction where the map suggested that Port Royal was nearby.

I saw a farmer walking a horse, and so I slowed to a stop a safe distance away from both human and animal. "Excuse me, sir," I said, out the car window. "Could you point me in the direction of Port Royal?" Without saying a word, he gestured toward the right-going fork in the road, and we then drove on a half-mile or so in that direction. It was almost uncannily easy: I saw on the near horizon a few farms and pointed to one of them, holding above the steering wheel the woodcut illustration so that my friends could also see it. That's the farm, we agreed.

It was about suppertime as I drew the car to a stop. The sun was beginning to set. I parked on the road below the house. There we sat awkwardly, talking among ourselves like a group of nervous novices. "Well, what now?" one friend asked. "I'm not sure," I said. "Are you going up there?" "Should we all go?" "No, we can't do that." "Don't get out of the car." There we sat, debating our next move—*my* next move—until ten minutes passed and I began to feel that we looked conspicuous.

"He probably sees us down here. He's going to call the cops," someone said. "Then get up there and say hello!" said another. I finally got out of the car and walked up the stone steps toward the house. I remember fifteen or more stairs built into a sloping hill, but I could be wrong because it has been more than thirty-five years and I haven't been back since. Stepping finally on to the porch, I reached the door and knocked quietly. A minute went by, and then it opened. Berry's wife, Tanya, was standing in the opening. I knew it was her. Anyone who has read her husband's poems and essays would know Tanya on sight, particularly as she was standing in the doorway of their home.

"Hi," I said, "I'm sorry that we're sitting in front of your house. It probably looks strange." I motioned down to the car. I think my friends were waving meekly from the windows.

She didn't say anything. She gave me a look as if to say that this was brand new, and that she had not noticed.

I went on, "We're college students from Chicago. I'm just a fan of your husband's. Could I possibly say hello to him?"

She smiled a generous smile. Then she said, "Oh, that's unfortunate. He is not here. In fact, I think he's in Chicago doing a reading tonight."

Since then, I haven't read all of Wendell Berry's more than eighty books, but I'm sure I have read at least half, and half of those I have read several times. I like the novels; I love the poetry, particularly the "Sabbath poems" that he has written for decades on Sundays; but most of all, I read and reread the essays. There is always movement in Berry's sentences. He writes about what he has experienced, what he has learned, with humility for what he does not know. Always humility for what is not known. The natural world is his primary teacher: its rhythms, its largesse, its mysteries. I grew up feeling drawn to birds and trees and mountains and streams, but without many real opportunities to get to know those things.

In Berry's essays, the natural world often shows or reflects how change in humans is also natural, inexplicable, and possible. I think this is what many who love his writing appreciate most, whether they realize it or not. At the time of my introduction to him by Mary Lou Kelly, I was reading William Wordsworth in high school and lines from "Tintern Abbey" were in my psyche:

> ...a wild secluded scene impress
> Thoughts of more deep seclusion

One experiences this again and again in Berry: a turning toward reflection that is borne apart from worldly things. So there is movement toward the natural world outside, and movement from those teachers back inside. We understand our desperate need for this pattern, and for places that might help it along. And a way of life that supports it.

For a farmer-writer, his world is not one in which spirit and matter are at war with each other. Instead, he points to human beings' poor decisions and bad habits. For him, the natural world is good; it is what we have done to the world that turns things bad. "We are living even now among punishments and ruins," he wrote in "A Few Words in Favor of Edward Abbey" (one of his own heroes).

I carried *Recollected Essays* for a long time. I carry it still. It does not so much help me find simple pleasures, but how pleasure itself is simple. It questions society's attempts to improve things, modernize, and always make life more efficient. Those words—improve, modernize, efficient—might as well be in quote marks whenever they appear in a Wendell Berry essay. He doubts them consistently. In a later essay, "The Way of Ignorance," he defines "arrogant ignorance" as "willingness to work on too big a scale." When life is lived more simply, those living it are apt to be more joyful, peaceful, loving, with basic needs satisfied, and in harmony with the land and its creatures. Provocatively, he writes, "Novelty is a new kind of loneliness" in another essay, "Healing." Specifically, he writes in "Horse-drawn Tools" that every machine or instrument designed for progress or increased efficiency "should be adapted to us [not the other way around]—to serve our *human* needs." This is exactly the conversation we are having now about mobile phones and how they are ruining us.

With Berry in hand, I recall in college arguing with adults giving me advice on what to do with my life. We do this to our elders: quote our favorite authors to dismantle the elders' assumptions. At a time when I was advised to think big and imagine how I might do great things, Berry's vision for what was great and good was the opposite of big. He wrote about the values of staying put (he'd left a teaching position at NYU to return to the Kentucky family farm), nurturing a small piece of earth with the passion and attention most people only bring to a career, and opting out of "progress." Similarly, at that time I remember reading a Lawrence Ferlinghetti poem called "Autobiography" that began, "I am leading a quiet life..." My elders could not understand this. I'd been told not to be quiet or inconspicuous, because that was in contrast to doing great things.

I want to live a small life. By living small and purposefully, I think I can do the most good, I would say. It was a Kentucky farmer-poet I was parroting. In these ways he sounds quite conservative, and in the early seventies when his children's generation were hippies, he was poking fun at the new conformism. He wrote in an essay, "Think Little," in 1972: "Individualism is going around these days in uniform, handing out the party line on individualism." Then he basically predicted that hippies would become Baby Boomers: "Our model citizen is a sophisticate who before puberty understands how to produce a baby, but who at the age of thirty will not know how to produce a potato."

That smallness of life is what has also drawn me, again and again, toward monasticism. I discovered later that Wendell Berry was a friend of Thomas Merton's, when Merton's books almost carried me into the monastery not far from Berry's family farm, where the two of them had a picnic at least once, joined by Denise Levertov, according to photographs taken by Ralph Eugene Meatyard. And when Berry writes in "An Entrance to the Woods" these words, I understand perfectly:

> Nobody knows where I am. I don't know what is happening to anybody else in the world. While I am here I will not speak, and will have no reason or need for speech.

These are just a few themes in Berry's work. There is also much on the value of hard work, the meaning of human dignity, the scar of racism in the U.S., buying local, and eating local. In fact, it is Wendell Berry who first said, "Eating is an agricultural act." ("The Pleasures of Eating")

He was not always right. Any writer worth carrying, I would come to realize, will anger and annoy you from time to time. He could be cranky, and I knew it from the start. I liked that about him—he did not seem to worry about always pleasing people. But his wisdom, and his call to better habits, and a better way of life, has formed me. At least I hope it has. I ended up choosing a quiet way to live, or at least on most days it is like that. Because no one writes and publishes books to go unnoticed, yet, writing must be one of the most inconspicuous forms of public life.

"The Berry Farm," watercolor by Kristin Searfoss (a friend in the car with me that day)

CHAPTER 6

MONICA FURLONG'S *THOMAS MERTON* AND HOW TO RUIN A HONEYMOON

SHOULD HAVE known better than to carry an intimate biography of my hero into the car and onto the plane of my first honeymoon, especially since in the couple years leading up to the engagement I'd been carrying it, and lots of other books by and about Thomas Merton, back and forth to the Abbey of Gethsemani in Kentucky. Flirting with the idea of a monastic vocation. Which means that having Merton in my bag was roughly equivalent to carrying on an affair.

In the opening chapter I told the story of a book that bridged my unhappy first marriage to my more mature second one. This chapter returns to that original marriage with an instance of how a book can be closer to us than a spouse.

Had I been more self-aware, I wouldn't have carried it. Or, perhaps, I was so unconsciously aware of who I was, that Monica Furlong's *Thomas Merton* was a lifeboat during what turned out to be a marriage lasting a rather long time—seventeen years.

Merton was my first real love. A world-wise and world-weary young man who experienced Europe between the wars, lost both his parents, was booted from Cambridge University for misbehaving, and then became big man on campus at Columbia, only to realize how vapid he was. He was urbane, easily infatuated, gregarious. He wrote poetry and novels. Fancied himself a radical. But, one day, he began a dedicated search to find his true self, and to the surprise of all his friends, the looking took him behind the walls of a monastery devoted to manual work and rigorous silence in the woods of Kentucky.

I was only twenty-one, which used to be considered an ideal age at which to either get married or join a monastery. So, when his biography was in my shoulder bag on that airplane, its presence was about more than what to look at while nodding over the Atlantic.

In my hands, this Thomas Merton hardback was the perfect thickness; its dust jacket in its original state, protected in a mylar sleeve. (I'd recently purchased a box of mylars for those jacketed books I wanted to carry.) And the photo of Tom on the front—it was as if he was winking at me. Thirty-five years later, I now write and edit books about the famous monk, and have done so for a long time. When I recently gifted one of these, with a warm cover photo of Tom, to a Catholic novelist friend, she said thank you followed by, "He was *so* sexy!" Maybe so. It was his life that appealed most of all to me.

We were like children on that honeymoon. We flew from Washington Dulles to London Heathrow and stayed the first two nights in the great city. I would remain up late each night, reading Furlong's biography, finding Thomas Merton more enthralling than ever, and at the most inappropriate time. I remember one evening when we had tickets to The Shaftsbury Theatre in the West End to see Anthony Hopkins starring in "M. Butterfly," I'd been awake so late the night before with my book, using jet lag as an excuse, that I fell asleep in the middle of the second act. Hopkins was brilliant, but I couldn't keep my eyes open. I awoke before the third act began, then fell asleep again.

There was an unquiet murmuring in my heart: *Is this who I am, this married person? Or, have I not found the real me?* The English Romantic-era writer, Charles Lamb once described silence (with hyphenated lines like an Emily Dickinson poem) as "eldest of things – language of old Night – primitive Discourser"—and we usually seek to escape those quiet-noisy moments when they're about to challenge our made-up mind. It was quiet as could be on that trans-Atlantic flight, on that honeymoon, in those first few months of marriage.

Each evening, rather than consumed with love and interest in my young bride, I was wrapped in an interior dialogue brought on by the book I was carrying, as well as by my silent feelings and desires. (Equally as inappropriate, I remember, years later, when we had two young children, what books I was reading while we were together on vacation in Maine. They were all in the pool, splashing; I was really somewhere else.)

Day three of the honeymoon, we rented a stick shift car and started our drive to Hay-on-Wye, the original international book town in Wales. To that haven, it was my idea to go. To that wonderful bookish place, I have never been back. What a shame I was there in a fog of many-aspect confusion. All I remember clearly is carrying Furlong's *Merton*, wondering who I was supposed to be.

A book can open up a part of us that might not ever open otherwise. Merton did that to me, and it became like a wound I salved with more Merton. I think it was in her autobiography, *The Gastronomical Me*, where M.F.K. Fisher laughed over an anecdote from the life of Walter Scott, telling the story when, as a young boy, Scott praised his mother's delicious hot soup only to have his father overhear the exclamation and then pour cold water into the boy's bowl. This was the conservative religious mind at work, saying that food was not to be sensuous, only eaten. Well, this marriage of mine felt from the get-go like dutifully eating my soup, when what I wanted most was elsewhere, and might always be.

I filled the void through books and then more books. In fact, eleven years after reading her biography of Merton on my honeymoon, and cofounding a spirituality book publishing house in

Vermont, I tracked down Monica Furlong in London. I pitched her an idea for a book: a collection of prayers by women that cuts across ages, faiths, cultures, and traditions. A beautiful hardcover. She had just turned seventy, but got straight to work, and although cancer took her in 2002, just three months after *Women Pray* published, the book was a success. It's still in print more than two decades later.

Who am I? is the question we all ask, and often fail to answer. I am still asking.

According to Merton, pride and other forms of sin are a kind of clouding, a taste for what is false, an ignorance and laziness. There are several rounds—hence, the "seven storeys" of his famous autobiography, *The Seven Storey Mountain*, which he wrote in the monastery at age thirty-three—where we see him clouded, false, ignorant, and lazy, again and again, in Cambridge, at Columbia, in Greenwich Village, Cuba, and elsewhere, even inside his beloved cloister. He confesses his pride, particularly in the struggles he tells and exhibits, even against his will, of trying to be more a Christian and a monk than a writer. This theme returns over and over again and is still there near the end of his life. As he confessed in his autobiography, "By this time I should have been delivered of any problems about my true identity.... But then there was this shadow, this double, this writer who had followed me into the cloister. He is still on my track. He rides my shoulders, sometimes, like the old man of the sea. I cannot lose him."

Ultimately, this is why I love Merton: his pride is not overcome. The uncertainty of life's meaning and ourselves remains, as they should, because maybe there is no true self and maybe we're just being honest.

CHAPTER 7

FINDING TAGORE
IN HARVARD SQUARE

T TURNS OUT that most of the books I have carried are wrapped in a kind of melancholy. I do not find on my shelves now many volumes that radiate happy associations. Perhaps this is a symptom of my personality. French writer, Michel Houellebecq, with whom I'd like to think I have nothing in common, believes "Those who love life do not read. Nor do they go to the movies, actually. No matter what might be said, access to the artistic universe is more or less entirely the preserve of those who are a little fed up with the world."

Or maybe the books of adulthood simply tend to resonate varieties of wistful sadness more than they do joy.

This story is about the first job I really loved, living in an unfamiliar place, the use of mass transit and walking in the city, and becoming a father for the first time. It is also about discovering the Bengali poet and Nobel Laureate, Rabindranath Tagore.

"Ta-gor-ey," I called him, the first time I said the name out loud. My co-worker at the bookstore where I was working in Cambridge, Massachusetts was fifteen years older than me, and had much more experience than I with the religions of the East. I was a straight white Protestant Christian seminary dropout from the Chicago suburbs who'd landed serendipitously in Boston. We were there first and foremost to look after my young first wife's cousin's dilapidating house on the North Shore. My bookstore colleague, Beth, had at least worked in the New Age bookshop in Harvard Square. She said very kindly that day, "I think it is actually pronounced 'Ta-gore.'" She didn't think it; she knew. I had never before said the name out loud, and had never before heard it said by anyone else. It was the novelist Jean Rhys who once remarked that reading "makes immigrants of us all. It takes us away from home, but more important, it finds home for us everywhere."

This was 1991. There were twenty-five bookstores in and around Harvard Square then. Twenty-five bookstores in one square mile. I was lucky to be managing one of them.

The young wife and I arrived in Boston and moved into that rundown, abandoned house three blocks from the shore of Massachusetts Bay in the city of Lynn, and I went looking for a job in bookselling. At twenty-four, I already had a resume of three years bookselling experience at two shops in Chicagoland, one used, the other general trade and textbooks. So I was hired, lucky that they needed someone, and in the era when bookstores hired staff full-time. Then, it turned out the manager was quite incompetent, and was fired two months into my tenure. I was given the keys. I remember Beth, who had been working at the store for several years already, said, "I have too many other things going on, outside of work. You should manage things. I just like the bookselling." She was always kind.

We were on the second floor of an angular red-brick American Baptist church in Central Square, Cambridge, about a football field's distance away from the transit stop and the Harvard Doughnut Shop on Massachusetts Avenue. I would ride the Blue Line from the North Shore end-of-line evocatively called Wonderland, into Boston at Park Street, switch to the Red Line in the direction of Alewife, and detrain one stop before Harvard Square.

An alewife is a fish, I learned from reading Thoreau, in one of the books I carried on my morning commute. I loved the train and the opportunity it afforded me to read. For those forty minutes each morning and afternoon, I had no other responsibilities. Packed in tightly, shoulder-to-shoulder on my orange plastic seat, I felt free. It seemed in those days of mass transit that everyone across, beside, and above me was holding a book or a newspaper. The newspapers were filled with daily atrocities from the war in the former Yugoslavia. I would glance at the headlines, and a few paragraphs over other's shoulders, before returning to the grace and simplicity of my more local reading. I enjoyed imagining that I could see some of what Thoreau saw if only I stayed on the train to the end of the line—the Alewife stop—and then walked the fifteen remaining miles to Concord.

Our eclectic bookstore in Central Square was devoted to the religious, justice-loving, theological, and spiritual. I was made for it. Since the age of thirteen I had caddied, sold shoes, waited tables, worked as a teaching and research assistant, and gone to college and seminary, but when I found bookstore work, I realized I had a calling. The first bookselling job was shelving inventory and running the cash register at a used and rare theological specialty store in our college town. The proprietor gave me a choice on day one: "I'll pay you six dollars an hour in cash, or eight dollars an hour in books." It was the easiest decision I ever made. I'd spend each day, between customers, making the delightful but difficult decisions of what to carry home when the shift was over. That first day, it was the first two volumes of David Knowles' *The Religious Orders in England.*

A second bookstore job came at the store across the street from my seminary on the northwest side of Chicago. Full-time graduate school was not a possibility, given the necessities of paying the rent and such, so I looked to keep working in books. I started as the book buyer and soon became the purchasing manager. They even sent me on a plane to my first convention: the American Bookseller's Association annual gathering in New York City. I was twenty-two and giddy, which seems odd now, if and when I walk the aisles of the Javits Center. In the evenings, instead of attending workshops or dipping into the free cocktail parties, I walked down to The Strand ("18 miles of books") in Greenwich Village and searched it like so many floors of paradise.

By twenty-four, family and friends were asking what I was going to do with my life. I thought it was obvious. They disagreed. I had friends and former classmates from high school and college who were finishing medical school, clerking for judges, working the Mercantile Exchange in Chicago, and junior staffers on Capitol Hill. Another was preparing a run for state office and would, a decade later, run for the U.S. House of Representatives and win. By contrast, my life seemed small.

The store in Central Square Cambridge was called Divinitas Books, founded a few years earlier by two recent graduates of Harvard Divinity School. Our primary work was to serve up the textbooks required at Boston University's School of Theology, Boston College's Summer Institute, Weston Jesuit School of Theology, and Episcopal Divinity School. Except for days each year when I had to carry multiple forty-pound boxes of textbooks up a flight of sixteen stairs, from the office to the sales floor, I loved my job.

Bookish environs stimulated me, and not only in my little store. Two or three times a week, at lunch, I would walk swiftly to 8 Mount Auburn Street, close to Harvard Square. One of the best used bookstores in the world, McIntyre & Moore, was there then. Google maps tells me now that it was a seventeen-minute walk. I used to do it in fifteen flat, because I was on lunch break. A half-hour of walking would leave me thirty minutes to browse and perhaps buy.

Curious oddities, too interesting to be shelved and obscured in their subject category sections, sat on little wooden stands on filing cabinets, behind which Messrs. McIntyre and Moore sat amid piles of papers and catalogues and stacks on the floor. It was on one of those wooden stands that I saw it. *Poems*, Rabindranath Tagore.

I'd spent enough hours in used bookstores in Chicago, New York City, and elsewhere to know that the little hardcover printed in Calcutta with Tagore's photo in black and white, was special. The paper of the pages felt different, looked a bit different. The frail thinness of the rumpled dust jacket was different too. And I knew that the fact it was inscribed on the flyleaf by someone to a friend, "To dear, dear Ellen from Berssenbrugge," soon after publication, "India, 16 June '45"—added to its lure and authenticity. Could this be Mei-mei Berssenbrugge, the Bollingen award-winning poet born in Beijing who grew up in Boston in the fifties? Not quite, but I wonder now about those connections. The book that day was nine dollars and quickly mine.

There are many things I would learn about the little volume later when I began to make studying Tagore a regular habit. When I read his best biographer, Krishna Kripalani, he referred to that book and his involvement with it. Sure enough, all those years later, I open *Poems* from my shelf to look for tiny print on the copyright page: "Edited by Krishna Kripalani in collaboration with Amiya Chakravarty." I had no idea then, also, that Chakravarty was one of the most gifted Indian poets and scholars of the twentieth century; and he, too, was Tagore's friend. I would soon also discover Chakravarty's friendship with the Catholic monk and writer, Thomas Merton, who was finding his way into my life also at that time. I did not know any of this that day on Mount Auburn Street at McIntyre & Moore at lunchtime. I only knew that the book—the pages, printing, and dust jacket—seemed unique. I would not realize until a quarter century later that *Poems* was compiled by these two friends of the poet very quickly upon his death, appearing in India the following February.

There are certain books we keep on our shelves and return to again and again. They become an annual ritual in our lives that's almost religious. Sometimes I do not even read Tagore's *Poems* when I hold it now. It sits in my hand like a holy object. Instead, I turn it over with my fingers and palms and look again at the frontmatter. I turn some of the pages and remember where I have been in them in years past. One day not long ago, doing this somewhat meditatively, I realized that the publishing house which issued my *Poems*, Visva-Bharati, was the very one founded by the great poet himself. I hadn't paused to notice that before. I could not have known that before.

No wonder the book felt authentic that winter day in Cambridge in 1991 when I snatched it from its wooden stand as if it were a jewel on a beach of stones and only I could, for a moment, see its jewelness. I intuited that this was a book I needed to carry, that it would come to define or explain some important part of me.

With Tagore in my bag and my soul, I became not just a reader, but a follower of enthusiasms. First, I got his name right, learning to say it properly. "Ta-gore." Thank you, Beth, truly. Then, I began to talk about the Bengali poet everywhere I went. It seemed that about one in three New York City taxi drivers then represented the Bangladeshi diaspora, and as I was often in New York, and if I figured this out early in a ride, I'd ask my driver, "Do you like Rabindranath Tagore?" The image of their faces lighting up makes me smile still.

Tagore is to India and Bangladesh as Shakespeare is to English-dominant countries. His work is studied by every school-child from Gujarat, on the Arabian Sea, to today's Kolkata, on the Bay of Bengal. He did not live to see the separation of Bangladesh from India, in August 1947; but this explains why he is the author of the national anthems of both countries. A 1961 black and white documentary about him, directed and narrated by Satyajit Ray, one of the great filmmakers in history, opens with the scene of Tagore's funeral procession on the streets of Kolkata in 1941, and you would think it was Mahatma Gandhi, his friend, who had died. There are millions of people there to honor him.

When Tagore was born, Kolkata was the seat of the government of Great Britain in India, in the century of Britain's world dominance, and he sometimes supported English rule of his people. He said that they needed education more than revolution. So, for instance, Tagore sometimes criticized the spiritualizing of Gandhi's principle of *satyagraha*, writing on one occasion: "Passive resistance is a force which is not, in itself, necessarily moral. It can be used against truth as well as for it." The notion that Indians should sacrifice their educations, their families, their very lives for the cause of *satyagraha* was never acceptable to him.

The circumstances of his fame in the West are also intriguing, and usually forgotten.

When Tagore was starting a school in India, in 1912, he decided to sail to England to study the educational systems of the West. Another Indian mystic, Aurobindo Bose, has suggested that the reason for Tagore's trip to England was his physician recommending a sea-trip as an antidote to recover from a serious illness, although that explanation seems off. The poet was in London for an operation. But the truth was, Tagore frequently traveled abroad, and he had been spending time in England since the age of seventeen, when he took classes in English literature at University College, London.

He was carrying a volume of his Bengali poems that he'd begun to translate into English on the sea crossing. Every writer carries current work when they travel. When Tagore met in London, William Rothenstein, Tagore showed him these fresh English poems, and Rothenstein in turn shared them with William Butler Yeats, who then showed them to Ezra Pound. Yeats' enthusiasm led to the volume, *Gitanjali*, being published in England that very year. Then a year later, again at Yeats' urging, came the Nobel nomination. Tagore was the first non-European to win the Nobel Prize for Literature.

What a surprise it was to me, not long ago, reading some of his letters, that he wrote one to Pound in 1913, several months before he was awarded the Nobel, and the address from which he addressed that envelope was 1000 Massachusetts Avenue, Cambridge—precisely midway between Central Square and Harvard Square. Tagore was in Cambridge, after a visit to Chicago, and before returning to India, to lecture in Harvard Professor James Houghton Woods' Indian philosophy classes. I was walking briskly past his old residence when I carried my *Poems* that first day.

The Yeats enthusiasm was when Orientalism was at its passionate height. The mysterious and exotic man of the East comes to the West, pointing to lost or undiscovered mysteries! They treated Tagore honorably but also like a virgin, foreign object. An Indian writer couldn't be judged or seen simply by his words or verses, but by his image—seen as brown, foreign, exotic, and exciting. Photography was still in nascent forms, and the popular fascination with it to capture celebrities (which then included authors!) in Edwardian England, in Tagore's case, made him famous and memorable overnight.

Tagore disliked attention gained this way, realized the way a photo portends to realism, but is used just as often in myth-making. A "counterfeit truth," one critic calls it.

The great poet was in fact on his fourth visit to London in 1912, when the public imagined he'd just stepped out of the mystical Orient into Western Civilization. The first visit took place a full thirty-four years earlier when, as a young adult, Tagore arrived in Dickens' London and reflected, "Such a dismal city I had never seen before—smoky, foggy, and wet, and everyone jostling and in a hurry." So much for the glories of London over Kolkata. Two of Tagore's children, and his wife, had recently died in an epidemic, before that first visit; in other words, he wasn't young and he wasn't remotely naïve. Yeats and Co. embraced his poetry probably for the wrong reasons.

I carried Tagore's *Poems* with me everywhere for many years. For a time, looking at the Indian paper on which my book was printed, slightly yellow and a bit textured in the way that paper made from rags in the late Middle Ages in Europe was, I fantasized knowing Tagore better, visiting India someday, his native Bengal, and coming to know the places he wrote about, and the spirit of the people, more intimately. On August 19, 1913, Tagore wrote a letter from London to his old friend, the white Protestant missionary C.F. Andrews (who lived in India most of his adult life, doing what I only fantasized doing), lamenting how out of place he felt among the British: "I must, without delay, go back to that obscurity where all living seeds find their true soil for germination."

When, in 1997, I was flying to London for a publishing conference, I found the email address of William Radice, the most important translator of Tagore's poetry in the West, and asked if we might get together to talk shop. As if I could talk Tagore shop. To my surprise, and to his credit, Radice entertained the opinions and even the invitation from this young know-nothing, and then to my credit, I bowed out at the last minute, not wanting to waste the good professor's time.

But I kept carrying my *Poems*. I began to imagine that I might learn to read Bengali one day to understand them better. I mentioned this desire to the national buyer for one of the large retail bookselling chains while in her Alabama office on a sales call, and she, miraculously, exclaimed "I'm doing that myself right now!" Teaching herself Bengali. Imagine the odds, I thought to myself. I remember her turning around and holding up the book she had purchased to guide her, then handing it to me. But my efforts never really went anywhere. I kept carrying the *Poems*, but not the grammar and vocabulary.

Tagore is still one of the world's best-known poets, and in the East that term means something greater than a writer of verse. *Gitanjali* remains his best-known work and is still widely read. Its poems speak of God, the soul, and love in ways that other mystical poets such as Kabir and Gibran share. Its opening lines go like this:

> Thou hast made me endless, such is thy pleasure. This frail vessel thou emptiest again and again, and fillest it ever with fresh life.
> This little flute of a reed thou hast carried over hills and dales, and hast breathed through it melodies eternally new. At the immortal touch of thy hands my little heart loses its limits in joy and gives birth to utterance ineffable.
> Thy infinite gifts come to me only on these very small hands of mine. Ages pass, and still thou pourest, and still there is room to fill.

Tagore's success a century ago must have had to do with how the renderings of *Gitanjali* resembled the language of the King James Bible. For example, the opening line of the tenth part reads like this: "Here is thy footstool and there rest thy feet where live the poorest, and lowliest, and lost." The word "footstool" appears sixteen times in the KJV; it was never a common word in other texts and traditions. I wouldn't be at all surprised if the average English reader of poetries and scriptures then would have had trouble identifying select passages of *Gitanjali* as distinct from similar verses in their bibles.

Tagore was also a novelist, playwright, musician, visual artist, philosopher, and author of hundreds of short stories and morality tales. And my *Poems* have none of *Gitanjali*. As William Radice in his first *Selected Poems* of Tagore in the 1980s purposefully excluded all but one poem from *Gitanjali*, determined to show Tagore's literary, rather than religious, swami-like, merits—so too Krishna Kripalani was motivated, in the wake of Tagore's death, to introduce the poet in his wider vision.

In my 1945 *Poems*, I turn to verses such as this one, and it is timeless:

> The world today is wild with the delirium of hatred,
> the conflicts are cruel and unceasing in anguish,
> crooked are its paths, tangled its bonds of greed.
> All creatures are crying for a new birth of thine,
> Oh Thou of boundless life,
> save them, rouse thine eternal voice of hope,
> let Love's lotus with its inexhaustible treasure of honey
> open its petals in thy light.

It is now thirty years since I first happened upon it, and I can accurately say I have spent a lifetime with this little hardcover on my nightstand, in my backpack, on my desk. I have only published one article about Tagore over the years, a review of an exhibit of his paintings in New York more than a decade ago, but I remember the timing of that piece because I was recently married to my wife, Michal, and remember walking the exhibit and talking about Tagore and how it felt as if we were still getting to know one another.

I left that job in Central Square Cambridge just two years later, and only because a baby was on the way, my first child, who is now in her thirties, because it felt as if I needed to make a little more money. Not that publishing paid particularly well, but bookselling paid even less. So, I found a job on the other side of the desk and have remained there ever since. Still, I remember with great affection those days riding the train, curating a shop with what I believed the world needed most, and hurrying down Mount Auburn Street with quiet discoveries in my hands.

CHAPTER 8

TOLSTOY'S *TWENTY-THREE TALES* AND LEARNING TO WALK ON WATER

HERE IS A pilgrim path north of Boston on I-95, moving to Route 1 at Newburyport, and across the state line into New Hampshire for the short but picturesque distance to Portsmouth where there used to be some of the most eclectic secondhand booksellers in New England. Sometimes the road would beckon to continue north to Down East Maine as well. This was my path on many weekends in my early twenties.

A bookstore, like an art museum, can be a spiritual experience—even a religious experience, with attention to ritual, text, and community. For two years, while living on the North Shore of Boston, this pilgrim path was my church on Sundays. I met Nobel laureate Joseph Brodsky in the narrow, well-appointed aisles of Much Ado Books in Marblehead one Sunday afternoon. I said hello to the poet Charles Simic at Sheafe Street Books in Portsmouth, simply because I found him browsing there.

After Portsmouth, you would continue on U.S. Route 1 across the Memorial Bridge into Kittery, Maine and the short distance to the near-beach shops in Wells and the warehouse-like Carlson & Turner Antiquarian Books in downtown urban Portland. On the way home to north Boston, you might stop in Ogunquit to eat at

Barnacle Billy's on the harbor. Never mind that I had very little money at the time. I had credit cards.

This chapter is about miracles in books and how there's nothing like a book to deliver these possibilities in human lives. "A genuine work of art must mean many things…. It is there not so much to convey a meaning as to wake a meaning," wrote the Scottish spinner of fairy tales, George MacDonald. It is also about how we have tucked books in our cassock pockets since before the printing press.

I remember how startled I was the first time I found the tiny blue cloth Oxford University Press hardbacks in "The World's Classics" series at Sheafe Street Books. They huddled together in a tidy row on a shelf near the front door high above the cash register. They are so small and yet so chock-full. Notable for their diminutiveness—just six inches tall and less than four inches wide—as well as for the clarity of their type design, they truly fit in a blue jeans pocket and yet hold together like a book printed in Oxford at the University Press.

There on that high shelf was *War and Peace* in three little volumes, just like nineteenth-century novels were supposed to be published. Likewise, *Anna Karenina* sat there in two. And they were both reprinted this way into the 1940s and '50s. But it wasn't those novels that captured my attention the first day—it was another Tolstoy in the row with a hyphenated title spine; I like oddities such as hyphenated titles, but also, I'd never heard of it. This is what I saw, looking up at tiny dark blue spines all in a row (sans jackets—booksellers nearly always tossed the jacket into the trash at the cash register when selling them new):

Twenty-
Three
Tales

——

Tolstoy

Oxford

Religion has lost its power for stories and storytelling. The narrative is broken and the mythos is largely evaporated. Stories are what have always preceded and seeded faith, but in most traditions the living communication of personal experience has been dampened by way too much didactic teaching. Still, stories are where religion began/begins. Before there was Torah, there were Jews telling stories, and then telling stories about stories. Before there was Gospel, there was Jesus speaking in parables and preaching by the Sea of Galilee, followed by his friends telling other friends what they remember hearing Jesus say. Isn't it interesting, though, that none of them decided to write any of it down? I remember reading once that Mani, the most fascinating of heretics in third century southern Mesopotamia, faulted Jesus for never writing down his teachings. Mani wasn't comfortable with oral transmission, at least not in religion.

Spoken tales are what creates the tone, conveys the message, and communicates character. Once catechisms are formed, we often go looking for new and different stories. And the people who write catechisms are probably incapable of really understanding the stories. Rarely are hearts moved by doctrine, but they are moved easily by stories that strike, like smoldering sticks on fresh kindling. Then they warm and illumine us. We see their light and are able to imagine once again our lives participating in their ardor and glow.

Storytellers are inspired ones. They often supplant, not supplement, the work of priests, rabbis, and imams. "The best thing you can do for your fellow, next to rousing his conscience, is—not to give him things to think about, but to wake things up that are in him; or say, to make him think things for himself," said George MacDonald. That is how every great story is meant to pierce the hearts of its listeners/readers. Stories are also how religion is renewed, and *Twenty-three Tales* became that for me, just as, I would discover, it had done for many people before me.

I bought Tolstoy's *Twenty-three Tales* for five dollars, and it didn't leave my body, unless I was sleeping, for more than a year. I read and reread this collection of tales for children, fairy tales, and folktales re-told and found them speaking to my changing heart, which was exhausted by so much organized religion. College had taught me that Tolstoy was a radical, excommunicated by his Russian Orthodox Church for apostasy. In 1901, after writing most of the stories in *Twenty-three Tales*, Tolstoy replied to the synod that excommunicated him: "I believe in God, whom I understand as Spirit, as Love, as the Source of all. I believe that he is in me and I in him." His unorthodoxies were many. But with a prescient form of what decades later became known as post-liberal, postmodernity, Tolstoy remained faithful without dogma, saying once to a scholar of the Gospels:

> What do I care if Christ was resurrected?... So he was resurrected—God bless him! What's important to me is the question of what I am to do, how I am to live.

And like the Buddhist who teaches, if you see the Buddha on the road in front of you, then kill him, Tolstoy said:

> God is for me that after which I strive, that the striving after which forms my life, and who, therefore, is for me; but he is necessarily such that I cannot comprehend or name him. If I comprehended him, I would reach him, and there would be nothing to strive after, and no life.

Caught up in its simple, radical truth, I went looking for more copies to give to quietly rebellious religious friends. I had many of those. We shared a crisis of belief and a disinterest in the opposite. Like Tolstoy, organized religion was getting in our way, as was the sterility of modern scholarship, too often separating us from the purpose of it all: to create a paradise of love and community on earth. That's what Tolstoy wanted to do.

Several years after my first encounter with that little blue hardback, I went with it on retreat to a midwestern monastery. I was to spend time in the monastic community, but most of all, to see a friend who was a monk there. He'd been at the monastery since his teenage years, starting as a novice working in the garden, before becoming many years later the community's abbot. After hours of intense conversation with my friend, I decided to leave him with my copy of *Twenty-three Tales*. He looked a bit puzzled. Why was I leaving him Tolstoy? I said that I thought he needed it. He ended up leaving the monastery just eighteen months later. I never asked if the little blue book had something to do with his decision.

Tolstoy composed his versions of the Russian folktales after years of soaking up legends of his native Russia. His biographers tell us how he often invited guests to his home, always to talk religion and philosophy, and how he listened carefully when stories were told. He also revered and observed the lives of ordinary men and women, peasants and serfs, pondering why they seemed to be happy regardless of their station in life, lack of formal education, or hapless circumstances. This was when he turned from the intellect (mostly Schopenhauer's philosophy) to the heart. He became interested in living a life of simple piety, modeling himself after the lives of ordinary people he knew in the countryside, or who worked on his rural estates, far from the life he'd previously thrived in, in St. Petersburg and Moscow. In 1870, the year after publishing his first masterpiece, *War and Peace*, Leo reflected in his journal, "As soon as man applies his intelligence and only his intelligence to any object at all, he unfailingly destroys the object." So he determined to make his faith simpler, based more on trust than doubt. He quieted the intense religious and spiritual questioning that had characterized his life. Not that the questions ceased, but they were quelled by the greater movement of his heart, welling up around the passions, emotions, and spiritual practices. Thus, by the late 1870s, he seems to have begun to know God personally.

Tolstoy began to attend mass, take communion, fast regularly, and he sought out his brethren rather than single himself out from them. He learned from Pascal that religious practice, done faithfully and honestly, can create true faith where before there was only the struggle to reason oneself to God. He began to acknowledge that happiness and philosophical speculation don't usually go hand in hand, and that in the gospels Christ praised the simple faith of children. Tolstoy expressed this in the strongest and most personal of terms: "If Christian teaching and love (which I hate, because it has become a pharisaical word) leads to people calmly smoking cigarettes and going to concerts and theatres and arguing about Spencer and Hegel, then the devil take such teaching and love." Faith and happiness well from the heart, and Tolstoy wished for that grace.

While publishing his second masterpiece, *Anna Karenina*, in 1877, the religious crisis was at its most intense. A sensitive reader can feel this in the final chapters of *Anna Karenina* itself. Tolstoy was seeking a more authentic, intimate relationship to the Divine. Following that novel, the stories and folktales of *Twenty-three Tales* became part of the spiritual outpouring of his interior life. No one who knew him or saw him during those years could mistake his passion. He was in both his interior life and external appearance, very much a pilgrim.

It remains unclear how original Tolstoy's versions of the stories and folktales are, and how much they were learned from others. Like all tales, they have a provenance that's ultimately impossible to trace. There's no question that an evangelical zeal accompanies them in the Tolstoyan forms. I was drawn to them for that zeal, and also for how they present religious life as most

MY LIFE IN SEVENTEEN BOOOKS

vital in expressions of ordinary, non-clerical people. It's no acci-
dent, for instance, that you can find today Tolstoy's *Twenty-three
Tales* reproduced in total on the websites of both The Anarchists
Library and Marxists.org.

Most powerful for me is "The Three Hermits." I once knew
it by heart, having read it so many times on those small pages. In
fact, I embellished my own versions—that's what we do with folktales—with my two eldest children at bedtime. Even as I baptized
and raised them in the church, I wanted them to imbibe a Tolstoyan
understanding of spirituality. I took Tolstoy's three hermits living
alone on an island in the middle of the sea and gave each of them a
task, to differentiate one from another. I would say:

> There once were three simple men who lived on a small
> island in the middle of a great sea. They lived there,
> together like brothers, for as long as anyone could
> remember. Each one had a long beard that reached almost
> down to his knees. Each also had a job he performed as
> a kind of prayer to God, and to help his brothers. The
> smallest man was a basket maker. The brothers kept their
> food in baskets, hanging them high in palm trees to keep
> away from animals. Baskets were also their beds, hung
> from tree branches as hammocks. So they needed a lot of
> baskets. The smallest man's shoulders hunched from the
> long hours it took to make each one, but he was always
> smiling. "Thanks be to God," he would whisper when
> one of his baskets turned out especially fine.

I was channeling my experience as a young adult in a remote
part of the Philippines, presuming to teach religious people how to
be religious differently. I was showing my children another way. So
I kept retelling Tolstoy's tale like this.

The story goes that a bishop, on a boat full of pilgrims bound for somewhere else, hears a local fisherman talking about three men who live alone on a passing island. Who are they? the bishop inquires. "They are holy men," answers the fisherman. Then he tells the bishop how one of the hermits "wears a priest's cassock and is very old," and how all three of them are kind, holy, and cheerful. The bishop's interest is piqued and he's also a bit suspicious. Men living far from church, sacraments, and the ministry of priests cannot possibly be as they are being described. He asks the ship's captain if they may stop, so that he can make a pastoral visit to the island.

A painful series of episodes commence, once the bishop is standing upon shore, finds the three hermits, and begins to question them. He asks them how they are working to save their souls. He asks them how they pray. He instructs them in the meaning of the Holy Trinity. The men are confused. After much lecturing, and the men practicing, they are finally able to recite the Lord's Prayer completely and correctly, until the bishop feels satisfied.

"It was getting dark and the moon was appearing over the water, before the Bishop rose to return to the vessel," Tolstoy relays. When he was back in the ship, "the anchor was weighed and the sails unfurled," and the ship returned to its course with the bishop standing on deck. He "sat alone at the stern, gazing at the sea where the island was no longer visible" when suddenly he began to glimpse something moving across the surface of the water. It was the three old hermits.

There they are, running "upon the water, all gleaming white, their grey beards shining," until they catch up with the ship, and with the ship still moving, the hermits call out to the bishop, "We have forgotten your teaching, servant of God."

To his credit, the bishop crosses himself, leans over the side, and replies, "Your own prayer will reach the Lord, men of God. It is not for me to teach you. Pray for us sinners." Tolstoy's point was clear:

That is the purpose of prayer, to change one's life, and the three hermits didn't need help from the institution.

My favorite professor in seminary, Paul L. Holmer, taught me how the words in our mouths make little sense without seeing the life of the one who speaks (or writes) them. He learned this from the philosopher, Ludwig Wittgenstein—who was also a Tolstoyan:

> It's not that a piece of language says everything it means; you can't read meaning off of words; and it isn't in virtue of the fact that you simply understand words that you know all that's meant; but rather, it's like this—that something about the form of life of the person who says the words *shows* you how the words mean. Not everything is said by the words; some things are shown you by the form of life in which those words take shape. The notion that one has to therefore know something about the form of life, and human forms of life, in order to understand words that are spoken, follows as a matter of course.

CHAPTER 9

SITTING WITH SWAMI
AND *THE GOSPEL OF SRI RAMAKRISHNA*

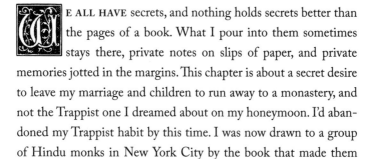 E ALL HAVE secrets, and nothing holds secrets better than the pages of a book. What I pour into them sometimes stays there, private notes on slips of paper, and private memories jotted in the margins. This chapter is about a secret desire to leave my marriage and children to run away to a monastery, and not the Trappist one I dreamed about on my honeymoon. I'd abandoned my Trappist habit by this time. I was now drawn to a group of Hindu monks in New York City by the book that made them known in the West, *The Gospel of Sri Ramakrishna*.

This remained a secret for good reason. Already I had friends and family who wondered why I strayed from my religious roots by going to work for a Jewish publisher. Then I cofounded a multifaith publishing house, SkyLight Paths, disconcerting more people who knew me from youth, college, and seminary days. *He's left the fold.* I'm sure there were those who believed I was an apostate. Still, my heart kept wandering, following, as it was, where books led me.

I'd briefly been a missionary as a teenager—which is a story I tell in some detail, below, in chapter sixteen. I'd been convinced of the need to convert even my co-religionists; I was a Baptist then, intent on making Christians out of Filipino Catholics. But instead, I was the one converted: to pluralism. It would be many years later, when I was exploring *The Gospel of Sri Ramakrishna* that I learned of the distinguished line of Christian missionaries in the middle decades of the twentieth century who traveled to India only to eventually abandon their Christian certainties—either entirely, or for a healthy pluralism. These include Verrier Elwin, who started as an Oxford-educated Anglican and ended up a Hindu practicing anthropologist. He fell under the influence of Mahatma Gandhi, as did C.F. Andrews, an Anglican missionary a generation older than Elwin who first encountered the Mahatma during Gandhi's years in South Africa. Gandhi called Andrews "Charlie," and would sometimes refer to him as "Christ's faithful apostle," riffing on his friend's initials. Andrews remained Christian, but developed close friendships with Gandhi and Rabindranath Tagore. Their published three-way correspondence is another book I treasure. In the great Richard Attenborough 1982 film, *Gandhi*, Andrews was played by Ian Charleson, who just a year earlier had starred as Olympian Eric Liddell in *Chariots of Fire*.

Then there was Bede Griffiths, who was a few years behind Elwin at Oxford, then became ordained in the Church of England, and later a Catholic priest and Benedictine monk. Bede went to India later in life, when Elwin had already been a Gandhian/Hindu convert for fifteen years. Like Andrews, Bede remained Christian, but was completely transformed by his real encounter with the East. And then there's the most fascinating of them all: Abhishiktananda, or Henri le Saux, also a Catholic monk, from Brittany, whose profound advaitic ("non-dual," meaning unity without distinction) experiences in the subcontinent completely blurred his Christian faith and practice, leaving it mostly unrecognizable by the end. Bede died in 1993, and Abhishiktananda in 1973. They both wrote many books and it is Abhishiktananda's that have yet to be understood.

I have never quite grasped the impact the Ramakrishna monks had upon me. I was able to spend significant time with them without it seeming too strange to others because I was publishing their swami. First, there was his book on meditation. Then a book on Vedanta as a way to peace and happiness. I acquired both books for the press, and saw them through to publication. These projects gave me ready excuses to visit their monastic community on New York City's Upper East Side two or three times a year, taking meals with them and talking about a wide range of interests and desires. It was a time in my life when I was stimulated by every new religious movement and person I met. Monks in ochre robes living in the heart of New York spending their days in meditation, study, service, and devotional acts was deeply appealing. I learned that these Ramakrishna monks were like the Jesuits of Hinduism: beginners spent nine to ten years as novices, the first two studying the Upanishads, Brahma Sutra, and Bhagavad Gita, with the commentaries of Shankara (their Church Fathers or Talmud rabbis all in one) at hand. I started my own self-study, and asked the swami many questions.

Two years into this association came an anniversary occasion at the Ramakrishna-Vivekananda Center and an invitation to participate in one of their religious services. I was invited by the swami to give a short talk. The occasion was the honoring of Holy Mother Sri Sarada Devi, the wife of Sri Ramakrishna, on her 150th birthday. While writing this chapter, I did a quick search online and, sure enough, one can find just about anything, including my presence there that day, which was April 23, 2004. I weighed ninety pounds more then, than I do now, so you'll see a much larger me in coat and tie on a dais at the end of a line of five Indian swamis: my host, Swami Adiswarananda of the Ramakrishna-Vivekananda Center of New York; Swami Tathagatananda of the Vedanta Society of New York; Swami Chetanananda of the Vedanta Society of St Louis; Swami Tyagananda of the Ramakrishna Vedanta Society, Boston; and Swami Yogatmananda of the Vedanta Society of Providence. While we sat meditatively (I, desperately trying to look like I somehow belonged), we listened for a half-hour to the chanting of the students of Vivekananda Vidyapith, which is an academy of Indian philosophy and culture across the Hudson River in New Jersey.

There were other notable people there, including prominent Upper East Side folks who had given a lot of money to support the Center, and professors, business leaders, and representatives of other faiths. I'm accurately described on that web page as "Jon M Sweeney, Editor-in-Chief, SkyLight Paths Publishing, Vermont, and author of *Praying with Our Hands, The Road to Assisi* and *The St Francis Prayer Book.*" When my turn to the podium came, I spoke for fifteen minutes on the Christian tradition of the Virgin Mary as the holy mother and the connection of this to what many had come to call the divine feminine.

Wistfully now, I remember those three years I spent pondering and meditating on *advaita*, the teaching of the Upanishads that the ultimate reality of God and the human being (in fact, all creation) are inseparable, and that spiritual maturity comes when one's individuality, goals, and purpose fade away into the ocean of that One. The desire to disappear was strong in me, religiously and otherwise.

It was *The Gospel of Sri Ramakrishna* that carried me there. I'd stumbled onto the book as a new copy on the shelf of The Seminary Co-op in Hyde Park, Chicago one afternoon at the tail-end of my seminary days. Not knowing what to make of it then, only that it drew me like a moth to flame, I put it on a low shelf with other large and heavy books and carried it from state to state, apartment to apartment. Its heft was surely part of its appeal; I've always been drawn to books of abundant pages as long as those pages are typeset with narrow margins, tight leading and kerning—my subconscious being satisfied to know that so much was poured into that vessel. This book is about 1,100 pages, printed on the finest paper with a slight gloss, like scriptures, but without the flimsy. And it has plates, which is what we used to call photographic illustrations, when they were produced using offset lithography on extra thick, very durable paper, designed to outlast your grandchildren. While writing this chapter I took my old copy to the baking scale; it weighs three pounds, nine ounces, about the same as a half-gallon of milk.

As you can see, I haven't mentioned the contents as yet. There's no question that they were secondary; I didn't even get to them for at least a decade. The book sat on my shelf all that time, unless I picked it up to admire its physical qualities, which included images of Sri Ramakrishna in *samadhi*—Sanskrit for "total self-connected-ness," or intense and ecstatic concentration, in meditation. As Rob Reiner's mom says in that scene in *When Harry Met Sally*, I wanted what he was having. But I knew I wouldn't.

They took me in with so much graciousness that I began to wonder and dream of joining them in New York. Remember, before I really read the text, under the swami's guidance, I'd begun that earlier quest to learn Bengali. Just as Rabindranath Tagore had written all his stories, poems, novels, and essays in Bengali, so too was *The Gospel of Sri Ramakrishna* "originally recorded in Bengali, in five volumes, by M., a disciple of the Master," as announced on the front cover of the dust jacket, and again on the half-title, of every copy printed. But Bengali never "took" in me. Love for Ramakrishna did, however, and when the Ramakrishna monks talked of him as a saint, the language made perfect sense.

The last I heard from my swami was a Christmas card in 2006. A beautiful color image of the emblem of the Ramakrishna religious order, carved in sandstone, from the entrance to the Ramakrishna Temple at Belur Math, India, was on the front. This emblem was designed by Swami Vivekananda, Ramakrishna's most famous disci-ple, who then led the Ramakrishna Order in the late nineteenth cen-tury. He's also known to history as the one who came to the Chicago Parliament for the World Religions in 1893, effectively introducing Hinduism to the West. He described the emblem this way:

> The wavy waters in the picture are symbolic of Karma, the lotus of Bhakti, and the rising-sun of Jnana. The

encircling serpent is indicative of Yoga and awakened
Kundalini Shakti, while the swan in the picture stands
for Paramatman. Therefore, the ideal of the picture is
that by the union of Karma, Jnana, Bhakti and Yoga, the
vision of the Paramatman is obtained.

I still don't know what some of this means. I probably never will. But
Vivekananda also became a passion of mine. In fact, it was while at
Every Other Book in Fort Wayne, Indiana that I found a special
copy of a rare Vivekananda volume in English, and tucked inside
was a typewritten letter from Swami Nikhilananda—who founded
the Ramakrishna-Vivekanada Center of New York in 1933, and
remained its leader for forty years—to the previous owner of the
volume. The letter began, "Dear Betty: I am glad to see that you
have become a Hindu missionary in the middle West. The seeds
that were sown here many years ago did not fall on barren soil."
Swami Nikhilananda had many famous students including Joseph
Campbell and Lex Hixon. I made a photocopy of the letter and
mailed the original to my friends in New York.

Back in Vermont, at my small publishing house, I asked the
brilliant Indian-born author, Andrew Harvey, to compile a book
of the best selections from *The Gospel of Sri Ramakrishna*. I knew
his love for the work. We had talked about it once at a conference
devoted to Bede Griffiths in England. That compilation remains
one of the books I published of which I am most proud.

My swami died about ten months later. I visited once, in the
aftermath, but the magic for me was gone. There would be no more
stopping at their place in New York, imagining what if.

All these years later, I haven't opened Ramakrishna's Gospel
in years, but there it sits, waiting, on a low shelf. I remain drawn
to unfamiliar scriptures and human beings' relentless pursuit of the
question of meaning and happiness. Most of all, I wonder if I was

ever truly close to leaving behind everyone I knew in order to don ochre robes of renunciation. It probably never would've happened, but the heart is a funny thing.

CHAPTER 10

HAND-HELD DEVOTION
(BOOKS WITH PICTURES)

 FEW OF these chapters tell stories of how I organize business and work around locating secondhand bookstores. This chapter is similar, except the bookstore wasn't secondhand and it came only at the end of a museum exhibit. I was there sneaking in a visit between marketing and sales meetings on a busy weekday in Cambridge, Massachusetts. I'm glad I did, because that day in The Fogg Museum at Harvard, in September 2000, altered forever how I entered the world—especially since I then had the opportunity to carry the book (the exhibit's book catalogue) in my shoulder bag for six months.

This story is about how a book can become a religious object, and it need not have religion or spirituality as its subject. Have you ever seen one of those Renaissance-era paintings depicting a person with a certain look on their face, gentling cupping their hands, that only makes sense when holding a book devoutly? The painter is imagining a breviary as the book, but it could just as easily be a novel or a how-to, if patterned religiously into one's life. This chapter is also about how pictures can make a book something other-wordly: passionate pages moving the heart, or feet, and stirring the emotions.

At certain books we are meant to gaze. We look at them differently than others. We take them in, more than read them. Before he could read English, Rabindranath Tagore came upon a book of Alfred Lord Tennyson's poems in his older brother's library, and the volume was full of the powerful drawings of Gustave Doré. Tagore said: "I wandered among its colored plates. I could make nothing of the text, but it nevertheless spoke to me in inarticulate cooings rather than words."

Such books can also become incendiary, and have been so, throughout history. The first publishers of books by offset printing, who were suddenly and speedily able to reproduce something a thousand times, were the first to practice the power of a picture saying more than a thousand words. My origins as a writer began with such books. I first wrote by imagining how words might combine with images to say more than words alone could do. Working with a professional photographer, I contemplated how hands are used prayerfully across spiritual traditions, and *Praying with Our Hands* appeared in 2000. In it, I offered, "Imagine the many emotions your hands already express: They can invite or beckon, repel or reject, hide or reveal, console or protect; they can embrace. When we pray with our hands, we are enfleshing the sacred—not just talking to God, or focusing our minds. In our hands, prayer becomes visible."

Then I began to research the origins of books, when scrolls became codices, how and why. This evolution took place over many centuries, but seems to have gained steam around the time of Second Temple Judaism, early Christianity, and the many gnostic sects when people had reasons for wanting to be able, finally, to carry their books with them in pockets.

A few centuries later, in Europe, came small devotional books, with scripture texts of psalms or Gospels and prayerbooks and the first litanies of the saints, and by the eighth century, they were often illustrated or illuminated. Illustrated means what you think it means, because we still have those in spades today. Illuminated means small bits of art, colorful flourishing, even doodling, at times, to add impact and spirit to the words on the same pages.

Such illustrated or illuminated books were designed to take the spirituality of a private monastic cell out into the world, to become available to any person anywhere. The poor little book was simply words on a page. These were something else entirely. And, ironically, a monk's vow of poverty was turned on its head with the artistic extravagance of some of these books. A monk's life may have been spare, but not his books. Ornamentation such as gold-gilded page edges could be expensive to produce, especially when they were treated as works of art to be created by paid artists. They were usually owned or commissioned by wealthy patrons. This is how the sixteenth century German artist, Albrecht Dürer, made his living. A very good living, in fact. He even successfully sued other printmakers for stealing his designs and monogram.

Not that I'm an art afficionado. Any true student or artist would shudder to hear me explain standing dumb for one short hour before gorgeous, original prints meticulously curated, framed, and annotated on maroon and green walls of The Fogg Museum, and then eagerly rushing to the gift shop to obtain the slip-cased two-volume work: essay and reproductions of each print. To see them on the walls brought me to a stop, to notice; but to carry those books, especially the album of prints, was like having God in my hands.

The truth is, I felt embarrassed viewing Passion prints mounted on walls with other people milling about, standing around. One young couple beside me as I contemplated the Flagellation was discussing where to go for lunch afterwards. There was a man in a nice suit glancing occasionally at his newspaper. I felt like a voyeur, at best, looking at prints that were designed to create believers. They were intended to be seen privately, as only a book can do.

Dürer's Passions. I first heard of both the exhibit and the book through a review by John Updike in *The New York Review of Books*. I still have his torn-out piece tucked inside my slip-cased volumes all these years later. Updike said: "Harvard's Fogg, having assimilated the old Busch-Reisinger Museum that once stood on the other side of Memorial Hall, has supplemented its own considerable holdings with some loaned prints to give us, in ninety-three works, the full array of Dürer's six [sic—he should have written "five"] versions of Christ's Passion—the successive events, from the Last Supper to the Crucifixion, of Christ's week of redemptive suffering." I knew right where that was, across Massachusetts Avenue and Harvard Yard from the Harvard Book Store.

I know now that the curator of the show at Harvard, Jordan Kantor, went on to finish his PhD and then moved to San Francisco where he's taught for nearly three decades. I come across his art criticism from time to time in *Artforum* magazine, but the topics are not religious anymore. His interests in prints and painting turned more to Jackson Pollock, Marlene Dumas, and Gerhard Richter, and I often wonder why. His essay in *Dürer's Passions* stirred me to the depths; how odd it would be if his words could do that, and he was writing from a place of no religious conviction whatsoever.

The print medium, reproduced in the *Dürer's Passions* album, was designed for private viewing. The advent of printed books suited its aims well. My *Dürer's Passions* guided my devotional practice for more than a year, and any book that holds our attention for a year or longer is both more than a book, and precisely what a signature book can be for us.

I've heard stories of other people carrying books with pictures into dangerous places, and as a way of protection, companionship, and comfort. There was the veteran I met who told me about a book of Sophia Loren trivia and photographs he had in his sleeping roll throughout a tour in Vietnam. And there was the young woman, finally removed from an abusive relationship, who told me she survived those years, in part, by always having nearby a travel guide to Paris—a place she's never been. There is magic to books with pictures that can attach itself uniquely to us.

Normally not absorbed in a Christian's maudlin appreciation of Christ's gruesome final day, these scenes of agony, scourging, mocking, humiliation, lamenting, and bleeding out nevertheless held me close. They are difficult to look at. Your eye wants to wander. On the museum walls, they were each about 5" x 3 ½", mounted very simply, just below eye level. Maybe the others were right—maybe it was best to glance at one or two and then start thinking about where to have lunch.

Man of Sorrows, Seated, from The Small Passion of Albrecht Dürer.
Wikimedia Commons.

It's the small details of the prints that captured me as I looked again and again, carrying the album in my backpack. There were thirty-seven in the series the artist called his "Small

Passion"—ranging from the Fall of Man (Adam and Eve with the serpent in the Garden of Eden) to the Last Judgment (the resurrected Christ prepared to judge every human being). This is precisely the narrative of life's meaning and course of salvation I've been trying to comprehend since childhood.

In the Garden of Gethsemane of the "Small Passion," St. Peter is there in the lower left-hand corner, hugging the sword he would use a few moments later, but for now, while Christ kneels and prays alone in agony, Peter's mouth is agape in full snore. Two scenes later, when Christ is being mocked, there's one mercenary holding the holy head down by his hair, another about to club him on the skull, and a third holding Christ's hands tightly from behind, grinning all the while.

In *Seeds of Contemplation*, Thomas Merton wrote, "For some people it is quite easy to return within themselves and find a simple picture of Christ in their imagination: and this is an easy beginning of prayer. But for others this does not succeed." I'm one of those others. I need books like *Dürer's Passions.*

But I suspect people used to look at these images differently than we do now. These were scenes meant to inspire repentance, perhaps awe, and to turn a gaze inward. They were part of the Christian practice of penance, which is not a popular practice in our time. I remember reading about how the Emperor Maximilian I, who was Dürer's patron and protector, when he died in 1519 left instructions to smash his teeth so that, when he appeared before God at the Last Judgment, he would seem penitent. I don't think anyone thinks that way anymore. But the artist's skillful cross-hatching on these woodcuts, so beautifully reproduced in the exhibit album, invites their contemplation and shows the contrasts between light and shadow as if there are layers of what might be seen from one moment, one day, to the next. And I can't stop looking.

CHAPTER 11

SIN AND MERCY
AT *BRIGHTON ROCK*

EMORIES FADE, and also betray us. I wrote another memoir once—more than twenty years ago now—and only realized several years after its publication that it was largely untrue. My research was deficient. I arrogantly assumed that I remembered things as they were. And I didn't do the interior work necessary to separate what was emotionally factual from what I wanted to be true.

On other occasions, I have experienced how memories simply aren't there, perhaps were never created, as if we go through some moments of our lives unconscious, unable to record feelings or memories of stimuli for future recollection. Is this why there are so many things I cannot remember clearly? Perhaps my lack of memory is because there were no books related to the business. Just as Teresa of Avila said she often needed a book in hand in order to start the inner machinery of prayer, I probably need a book in hand to start the machinery of, well, just about anything meaningful in my life.

There was no single volume in this case. But there was a stack of Graham Greene novels. I carried an elbows' length of Penguin paperbacks for years, reading them on trains and subways, tucking them in suitcoat pockets while walking onto airplanes. So this is a story about one author's vision, the meaning of religious conversion as a pursuit and pathfinding, lonely New England circumstances and the absence of supportive community, and my realizing how and why I ought to finally become a Catholic because I realized I already was one.

I obtained my deliciously-worn, previous generation Graham Greene Penguins for fifty cents a piece.

For a decade I was the volunteer organizer, sorter, and chief bookseller for our annual St. James' Church Fair on the Green in Woodstock, Vermont. St. James was my Episcopalian congregation, founded in 1827, housed in a Gothic revival building designed by Ralph Adam Cram with triptych Tiffany glass windows and original wooden kneelers. During my years at Anglo-Catholic St. James', the rector often celebrated mass with her back to the congregation, and we liked it that way.

Every July, at the height of tourist season, we would fill half the village green with books and other things for sale. We'd usually raise $20,000 or more in two days—the bulk of our annual budget for making donations in the community—with twenty-five percent of that total coming from my well-sorted piles of secondhand books. We began accepting donations three months in advance and I would pour over those bags and boxes of dusty volumes with pleasure. I can't say I ever found an Edgar Allen Poe *Tamarlane* or anything of real significant value, but I made many purchases from the piles myself—books that remain on my discriminating shelves to this day.

One year, a woman in the village who recently retired from secondary school teaching in Canada, donated much of her library, packed in twenty bank boxes, including a Penguin edition paperback of every Graham Greene novel. Most of them were published in Britain and bought by her when she lived up north. I knew this because I knew her personal story, but also because I understood how a Canadian bookseller would price such a book, and those little stickers appeared on most of the rear back covers.

United Kingdom 3'6
Australia $0.65
New Zealand $0.50
South A'
Canada 75c

Greene's *Brighton Rock* purchased new in Canada, ca. 1969

I was a faithful Anglo-Catholic then, which is how high church Episcopalians refer to themselves, indicating that they are both in practice and, they suggest, in history more Catholic than the Pope. (Wink and forget about Henry VIII and it almost works.) It was to the Episcopal tradition that I went when, after those years yearning for Trappist monastic life, I found myself married with children and a career. My wife was very much Protestant, and so were my children, as well as all my family of origin, so the idea of becoming a Roman Catholic was unthinkable then.

I didn't have the kind of doctrinal qualms that Simone Weil had when she wrote her famous *Letter to a Priest* in 1942. She was a more scrupulous thinker than I've ever been. I had concerns about papal infallibility and the First Vatican Council; I was worried, but mostly intrigued, about Catholic reverence of the Virgin Mary, until I spent a year writing a book about the BVM and Catholic lore of her and easily softened my stance. It wasn't about belief, for me. Conversion was ultimately more about identity, aspiration, and recovering a past, and I knew that every tribe and team has its problems. I was a religious pluralist before my conversion to Roman Catholicism, and I would remain a pluralist afterwards. Still, I carry Simone in my wallet:

> Faith. To believe that nothing of what we are able to grasp is God. Negative faith. But also, to believe that what we are unable to grasp is more real than what we are able to grasp.... To believe, finally, that what lies beyond our grasp appears nevertheless—hidden.

Graham Greene was unimpressed. "She talks of suffering 'atrocious pain' for others, 'those who are indifferent or unknown to me...including those of the most remote ages of antiquity,' and it is almost as if a comic character from Dickens were speaking," he wrote about Simone Weil, after her death, in 1951, referring to her attempts to champion the cause of the poor during World War II, when she essentially did little more than starve herself to death. "We want to say, 'Don't go so far so quickly. Suffer first for someone you know and love,' but love in these pages [of her writings, which he was reviewing] is only a universal love."

A Burnt-out Case and *The Heart of the Matter* are two of the Graham Greene novels that I recommend most often now, but it is *Brighton Rock* that remains in my mind most of all as I write all these years later. Perhaps that is because the film adaptation from 2011 became one of my favorite movies. I reviewed it for a magazine, upon first release, and then have seen it a dozen times since then. Like his younger contemporary, John Le Carre, to know Graham Greene's work is to know the film adaptations as well as the novels.

Sam Riley and Andrea Riseborough star with Helen Mirren in "Brighton Rock" (IFC Films), directed by Rowan Joffe, and from the ominous opening foghorn it's dark and foreboding. It's supposed to be. The novel—which I carried in my bag for years after reading it—centers around Pinkie Brown, a rail-thin gangster who doesn't just happen to be Catholic; being Catholic is central to his understanding of evil. Most of all, Pinkie is Catholic because he knows hell is real. And damnation.

An unrepentant murderer, Pinkie is one of Greene's extreme characters, devised to make the reader ponder. "It's not what you do," Pinkie says at one point, "it's what you think.... Perhaps when they christened me the holy water didn't take. I never howled the devil out." A few chapters later he says that, despite (or because) of his murderous heart, he used to want to be a priest. No longer religious, Pinkie would never call himself an ex-Catholic even though he was at the opposite end of practicing the faith.

I once wanted to be a priest too. I finished college early and started seminary at the age of twenty-one in order to become one. Until all of that fell apart. That: the sense of surety and safety I once felt with God. Within a few years of leaving seminary, I came to understand how Graham Greene might describe himself an "agnostic Catholic," even an "atheist Catholic" later in life. The religious Jewish writer, Rabbi Nachman of Breslov, taught that each word of prayer should be like a rose picked from a bush, creating a beautiful bouquet of praise. Seemed to me then that prayer, still one of my regular occupations, is more like picking roses from rose bushes that have dangerous thorns: you try to pray without getting pricked.

Pinkie is a menacing thug who has lost his father figure, the leader of his gang, murdered by a member of a rival gang. Pinkie is coping with this but also with the ramifications of his own revenge murder of the murderer. In the film adaptation, his facial expressions are a mix of sneer and the vacancy one associates with sociopaths. Once the revenge murder is done, the three other members of the gang insist that Pinkie obtain the only evidence that could link them all to it: a photograph taken on the boardwalk by an innocent vendor, given to an innocent girl. So Pinkie befriends the girl—her name is Rose—and obtains the photo, only to realize she already knows too much. So he woos her and courts her. It is plain and painfully clear to us that Pinkie despises her, is only using her, but Rose, innocent as she is, believes him.

"I love you" and "I'll never let you down," Rose tells Pinkie, and he responds with a mixture of quiet shame and contempt. Rose is Catholic too, and sincerely so.

"I'm one," Pinkie tells her on their first date. "Why, I was in a choir once." Then he asks her, "Do you go to Mass?"

"Sometimes," Rose says, then offering some excuses of when she finds it difficult to attend, due to work and other commitments.

"I don't care what you do," Pinkie responds, adding, "I don't go to Mass."

"But you believe, don't you?" she asks him, with concern.

He responds in a way that shows he is sincerely Catholic, as well: "It's the only thing that fits…. Of course there's Hell, Flames and damnation…torments."

She interjects, "And Heaven too." And Pinkie responds, "Oh, maybe, maybe." He shakes his head.

"But you believe?" she asks.

"Course I do," he says. "It's the only thing that makes any sense." He says that hell and damnation are what makes the most sense of all. His willingness to face damnation is a sign of his sincerity of faith.

The other pivotal character is Ida, who wants to warn Rose off Pinkie. Ida is irreligious, but good, in contrast to Pinkie's religious desire for damnation. Ida is a waitress in the novel but a manager of waitresses in the film, and dedicates herself to punishing Pinkie for the murder. The man Pinkie murdered was a friend of hers. Ida is far more promiscuous in the novel than in the film; Joffe made her secularly respectable whereas Greene made her only morally so. The narrator of the novel tells us that Ida and Pinkie have different views of death and life: "Death shocked her, life was so important. She wasn't religious. She didn't believe in heaven or hell. … Let Papists treat death with flippancy: life wasn't so important perhaps to them as what came after; but to her death was the end of everything." Pinkie, the killer, was just such a Papist. He committed a mortal sin and knew it. Ida knows it, too, but there seems to be nothing she can do about it.

In his efforts to keep Rose quiet, Pinkie is soon negotiating with her father, a despicable man, to marry her. He ends up paying the old man a dowry. Pinkie and Rose marry, but not sacramentally. No priest, no mass. She is late arriving. "I went to church," she tells him as she rushes into the courthouse. "I thought I'd go to confession," she tells him, but then she remembers there is no purpose in it because by not marrying in the Church they are sinning anyway. In the film, we watch Pinkie take Rose aside at this moment, with kindness or menace or both, saying, "You've got to understand: This isn't a real ceremony. This is sin, Rose…. There'll be no good going to a church ever again." A moment later, as they wed, Rose stands before a window with a ray of light upon her; Pinkie is all in the shadows.

If you've ever read it, you may remember the most quotable line from the novel, spoken by the priest who hears Rose's confession (although she claims that she didn't come to confess anything). She claims not to be worried about damnation or the future. He nevertheless offers her hope: "You can't conceive, my child—nor can I or anyone—the appalling strangeness of the mercy of God." There is good in all of us, perhaps more than we can imagine inside those who refuse the comforts of spirituality and sacraments, opting instead to remain outsiders, even to the extent of remaining outside the hope of what religious people call salvation. Forgiveness is especially possible for those who seem most willing to be damned.

It was not just Pinkie, but that old Canadian-bought beautiful pale paperback of *Brighton Rock* that pointed me toward joining the Roman Catholic Church. If it could hold and wrestle with a character like Pinkie, and the rebellious Graham Greene, it could surely hold me. But I'm also sure I wouldn't have gotten there had I been offered the hardback of the novel instead. Have you seen it, in the original pink dust jacket? It is the oddest thing, looking like a box of something from the grocery store. I wouldn't have given it a second look.

Instead, this comfort, of God in the shadows, is what made me feel ready to become a Catholic after so many years of deliberately not being one. I, too, frequently felt lost and agnostic. The story of Rose and Pinkie—so similar, so different, both human—were like a piece I found that had been missing from my puzzle. For a decade I had written books on Catholic subjects, including one in which I argued that the act of conversion itself was passe, such a twentieth century idea. It was by carrying Graham Greene's novel about Pinkie that, by strange mercy, I was shown a piece of who I was.

CHAPTER 12

A TINY VOLUME
OF WHAT'S IMPOSSIBLE

T BEGAN WITH simple greed, when I traded for this one. It wasn't quite the steal that my brother's black-and-white TV was, in 1979, when at twelve I convinced him to trade it to me for an Ahmad Rashad football card, but whatever those slightly rare Bloomsbury novels were which I exchanged with an Episcopal priest in 2007 for *The Mirror of Perfection*, I clearly got the better end of the bargain.

Just the other day, with curiosity I went online to see if I could find another copy and found only one that fits its description. This is how the bookseller put it, which I reproduce here verbatim remembering the college afternoons I spent working as a cataloger of rare and out-of-print theological and religious books:

> Hardcover. Condition: Very Good. Frontispiece (illustrator). Second Impression. London: 1899. (First published in 1898. Translated from the Latin; *Speculum Perfectionis*.) Hardback. Half title page: The Brother Minor's mirror of perfection to wit the blessed Francis of Assisi. Frontispiece. Original dark brown ribbed cloth; gilt lettered spine & cover. Top-edge gilt; other edges

untrimmed as issued. Ribbon marker. Bright, tight, and clean. No owner name or internal markings. Minor wear only. Very Good. (xvi), 231 pages. Index.

It was twenty years into my obsession with Francis of Assisi when this tiny book (4 3/8" x 6 3/8", less than 6.5 ounces) came under my roof. I knew the controversy surrounding it (more on that in a minute) in a way the Episcopal priest did not, and my life was wrapped a bit in those controversies in ways that the priest's could not have possibly been.

Being small was part of its bookhood for me. I've always been drawn to little books. When I am in used bookstores, I pause to look at almost every old, or odd, small volume. Just the other day I purchased duplicate copies of those terrific early New Directions "paperbooks" of Denise Levertov poems with sewn bindings because I can't resist their bookhood smallness. Little did I know, as a younger man, how loving little books was preparing me to appreciate Catholic piety. Prayer collections, saint's lives, novenas, books of blessings, and penny catechisms—all of these are found as little books. The seventeenth century poet Richard Crashaw once wrote 118 lines on the power of a little prayer book. These included:

You'll find it yields
To holy hands, and humble hearts,
More swords and shields
Than sin has snares, or hell has darts.

Their often-gilded pages repulse the clever people who often disparage things I enjoy.

Little books can go anywhere. They were once the most dangerous way to affect opinion and change, as when Martin Luther was picking fights with cardinals and popes in the early sixteenth century, quickly scribbling his little tracts. His Reformation—with Albrecht Dürer's help (see chapter 10)—was fueled by little books. For the decade or so when his life was in constant danger, Luther was always waiting anxiously for some tract to get off the press. He believed that each one would sway public opinion to his causes, and they often did. Erasmus also used little books—designed to entertain, with sarcasm, puns, proverbs, and other forms of wit—to fuel the Renaissance. He wrote what were called *Colloquies*, or entertaining short plays, used to teach and learn Latin, and he compiled many volumes of short proverbs from literature around the world. People laughed at Erasmus's little books, and he was glad. Luther once compared Erasmus to a slippery eel that only God could catch.

Ask your Catholic grandmother to turn her pockets inside out and you may find a rosary, but look on her night table and you'll find little books. The mass market paperback of today is a modern invention, but small books have always been around religious people. The average pocket of a pilgrim in Geoffrey Chaucer's day was more generous than a blue jeans pocket today, but the size of little books has, for the most part remained a constant 4 x 7 inches, give or take. What swam in the monk's cassock bulges a bit even in today's khakis. There are even tiny books that fit in the palm of an adult hand, such as my little *Mirror of Perfection*.

There have been many times in history when little books changed the world. Small booklets of prayers to the Virgin and reflections on the Magnificat of Mary were distributed among Cesar Chavez's farm-workers in the 1960s in California, and among Guatemalans in the 1980s. Or, consider the censorship trials of the twentieth century: D.H. Lawrence's *Lady Chatterley's Lover*, or Allen Ginsberg's *Howl*, both small books. It is rare today that people pay such close attention to the printed word.

The Mirror of Perfection frontispiece

In this country, little books really got going with Beadle's Dime Novels in the 1860s. These were adventure tales of the Old West, bank-robbers, Buffalo Bill and Kit Carson, and they soon had numerous competitors vying for an expanding readership. Nearly eighty years later, in 1939, Robert de Graff's Pocket Books were introduced at only twenty-five cents each. The cheap, disposable format allowed people to read it once and then pass it to a friend. The price featured prominently on the front cover of each one in type as large as the title. Film tie-ins were, from the beginning, a key to sales. For instance, Laurence Olivier is who really sold *Wuthering Heights*, not Emily Bronte. De Graff was often reprinting within a week of a book's release. Just as people have always bought little religious books outside of traditional bookstores—for instance, dropping coins for them into boxes in large city churches, or purchasing them while on retreat or pilgrimage—people bought Pocket Books in places that had never before sold books: cigar shops, subway newsstands, pharmacies.

When I was sixteen, I first encountered the life of St. Francis, and it was my ego and personae I discovered then, as much as a fascinatingly countercultural medieval man. All the preaching and teaching regarding sin and salvation I'd heard since childhood from the pews hadn't revealed to me the divine, eternal spark inside of me that my illusions had obscured. A book was needed. A medieval mystic would understand this in ways that an unreflective twentieth-century teenager would not.

My 1898 edition of *The Mirror of Perfection* was a product of the genius of Paul Sabatier, the writer who was the first to unearth the real Francis of Assisi, with a magnificent modern biography. That earlier book—the biography, *Saint Francis of Assisi*—is what I found at sixteen, and turned my attention to Francis for the rest of my life. Francis' life was a demonstration of what seemed impossible: following the teachings of Jesus in the gospels to the letter. Sabatier didn't create hagiographical fluff, but managed to show Francis as a real person, who in very human ways lived a divine life. It was a sensation when first published, translated into every European language within a few years, overturning centuries of sentimentality when it comes to saints, especially the world's most popular saint, which Francis quickly became. Sabatier applied the tools of modern literary and historical criticism to a subject previously thought too precious and fragile to withstand it.

I didn't find the biography—it wouldn't have been—in a bookstore, since all I knew then were bookshops selling shiny new titles. I stumbled upon it in our public library, in a carrel—those private-public monastic-like cells in libraries designed for discovery, where someone may find themselves in ways that couldn't happen elsewhere. Several years later I found my own copy at a secondhand book dealer and bought it for twelve dollars.

Paul Sabatier was a French Protestant pastor and amateur historian who respected the critical methods of late nineteenth century liberal scholars of religion such as Ernst Renan and David Strauss. For this reason, all of Sabatier's work went immediately onto the Vatican's Index of Forbidden Books. But unlike them, Sabatier was a historian who held on to his faith, just as surely as he applied the rigor of their methods of scrutinizing traditions and sources. It was that scrutiny that got him into trouble with *The Mirror of Perfection*.

I can't overstate the impact his work had on my own. My first book was the little project with a photographer I mentioned in an earlier chapter. I was then in the midst of co-founding a publishing imprint of multifaith and interfaith books and *Praying with Our Hands* was, in part, brand-building. That's how I justified it to my boss at the time. If he'd known of my desire to author more often, he would have been unhappy. I joined his firm for what would end up being a seven-year run that I remember mostly with fondness, but he was an old-world entrepreneur who demanded fealty like a taskmaster with a young apprentice. "His Secrets keep, his lawful Commands every where gladly do," is how the agreement read between Joseph Johnson, a bookseller in late eighteenth century London, and the boss with whom he was bound for seven years, George Keith. Conditions governing their relationship were strict and monitored. "Fornification and matrimony were both forbidden during the course of the apprenticeship, as were cards, dice, gaming, the selling of goods without permission, and the haunting of taverns and playhouses." Well, centuries pass, and the rules were only slightly different governing my employment. One of them clearly was: no meaningful projects outside work.

This is why, when a publisher in Scotland licensed the UK rights to my first book, I refused to allow them to put what is a standard line on a UK edition copyright page: "The moral right of Jon M. Sweeney to be identified as the author of this work has been asserted"—so worried was I that my employer back home would think I was trying to be a writer.

My second book was the creation of a re-edited edition of Sabatier's famous biography, with added sidebar notes and addenda, and a modernizing of the English translation. I called it *The Road to Assisi* and my publisher added: *The Essential Biography of St. Francis*—a bit haughty, sure, but it seems to have worked, since it became a selection of the History Book Club and Book-of-the-Month Club and sold about 100,000 copies in various editions. I was suddenly more than a publishing employee; I was a spirituality author. But I made up a story to tell my boss as to why it was necessary for me keep writing. He relented, but only slightly. A few days later, he looked me seriously in the face and said, "If you have time to write another book, that means I am not giving you enough to do here." So before my third book was advertised in a publisher's seasonal announcement catalog, I knew I'd have to give notice and find somewhere else to work.

The trouble that Paul Sabatier encountered in *The Mirror of Perfection* is an interesting anecdote in Franciscan historiography. As I say, Sabatier had established himself as the world's most important scholar in his field, and perhaps this went to his head, because when he found the previously unknown manuscript of *The Mirror of Perfection* he quickly made wrong-headed assumptions about it. A reformer and progressive radical, Sabatier was fond of the texts of fourteenth-century followers of Francis who painted a sour picture of life within their religious order, framing their own faithfulness to the movement's original ideals as a kind of lost remnant. Sabatier thoroughly believed these lonely and righteous friars' interpretation of events. They called themselves "Spirituals" and believed in absolute fidelity to Francis' teachings on complete poverty for every friar and every Franciscan institution, which meant there were to be *no* Franciscan "institutions." So Sabatier was quick to see what he wanted to see: that *The Mirror of Perfection*, which is full of sentiments marking the teachings of the Spirituals, must have been written by the friar who was most closely identified by Spirituals as their own, who was also one of St. Francis' closest friends while he was still living: Brother Leo of Assisi.

It turned out, though, that the *Mirror* did not date from the time of Leo. Just three years after Sabatier's 1898 publication in English, another scholar, who was also a Franciscan friar, demonstrated that the text could not possibly be dated earlier than 1277— which would be a couple generations after the time when Leo and Francis were walking together around the Marches of rural Italy, and several years after Leo was known to have passed on.

I knew none of this when I was first carrying Sabatier's work on Francis, and it wouldn't have mattered anyhow. I was a young man under the influence. Sabatier's biography portrayed the saint as a reformer of the church, spurred on by poverty, fighting against corruption with virtue—and this was the Francis I wanted to follow and who I dedicated my writing life to exploring and promoting. A rare photograph of Sabatier has hung in my office since my twenties, when I found it in another old book; it hangs there along with several St. Francis icons, photos, and a few other religious objects. Sabatier was determined to return to the original ideals of a Christian life: living in community with the poor, allying with those in need rather than the powerful, and finding joy in simplicity. Throughout the centuries, since Christ, attempting to live that way has been to fly in the face of power, progress, wealth, might, institutionalism, and growth. It's impossible, but necessary. Sabatier's Francis is thus at odds—or at least deftly avoiding—popes, cardinals, curia, princes, and armies.

Some historians have lamented his interpretation, saying there isn't enough evidence for it in the sources. Perhaps this is so, and I wouldn't pretend to be able to truly weigh-in except to say there's a reason why, in the words of one recent detractor, "Unfortunately, Sabatier's mapping of Franciscan history took hold," and that's because it rings true to what we know of the world. Those who try to live as Jesus did and taught, are usually tripped up by those who hold power or want "what's best for us." I'll take the Francis of Sabatier's telling every day of the week and have tried fitfully and mostly unfruitfully to model my actions in that mold.

It's simply a compilation of anecdotes and stories of a saint, *The Mirror of Perfection*, intended to show its subject as a "mirror" (*speculum*, in Latin), meaning, to be imitated. It's a genre of spiritual writing that goes back centuries, and there are examples of similar anecdote collections throughout the Middle Ages in the Christian West and East. These texts are always about showing, through story, the difference between who you are and who you ought to be. They are books for idealists, and they aren't exclusive to Christianity. There are similar story collections from Zen and Confucian traditions, in Japan and China, from the same time period. In fact, it was just such a book that carried me at the end of my first marriage, through stories of the early Hasidic Jewish masters. It's all about hope.

CHAPTER 13

CARRYING BARON CORVO
AND MY OWN PETTY ANIMUS

I PAUSE NOW at perhaps my favorite book of all. People ask that question when visiting your home and seeing too many books on shelves, floor, dining room table, near the toilet, and I never like answering. Feels supercilious, like responding to a child with my favorite color. But when I do answer, it is this, the one I reread every couple years and carry in my bag much of the time in-between: *Hadrian the Seventh*, Frederick Rolfe's fantasy papal novel of settling scores and revealing his own complicated, screwed-up life. It makes me feel better about the bad Catholic I also am, and about my own many problems. If we could all just write a brilliant novel that allows us to triumph over the inane, get even with our enemies, poke fun at our sins, and then die a martyr's death in the way that we once dreamed of doing as children.

Why read it—or any book—over and over? William Hazlitt may have expressed this best: "When I take up a work that I have read before (the oftener the better) I know what I have to expect. The satisfaction is not lessened by being anticipated. When the entertainment is altogether new, I sit down to it as I should to a strange dish,—turn and pick out a bit here and there, and am in doubt what to think of the composition.... In reading a book which is an old favourite with me...I not only have the pleasure of imagination and of a critical relish of the work, but the pleasures of memory added to it." That's how I feel.

When the Jewish philosopher Edith Stein converted to Catholicism, and was asked by Jewish friends and family why she did it, she sometimes responded with a Latin phrase, *Secretum meum mihi*: "My secret belongs to me." Eventually, she entered a Carmelite convent, upsetting her family even more. One of her nephews wrote decades later, "That was to us a dark, nocturnal aspect [of my aunt] which no one understood and which she neither could nor would explain to anyone." But I might understand what Stein meant by what she said. We are puzzles to others; we're puzzles to ourselves; and who we are is ultimately perhaps a secret. Frederick Rolfe was just as private as Edith Stein, even if more ornery about it. He prefaced *Hadrian the Seventh* with a Latin sentence on the title page: *Neve me impedias neve longius persequaris*, "Do not hinder me or pursue me further."

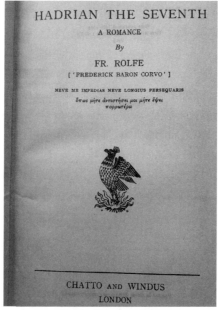

Hadrian title page, 1929

Sometimes one book we carry has another book to go with it. With *Hadrian the Seventh* is this novel's close cousin (you can't talk about the one without the other): *The Quest for Corvo*, a biographical investigation of *Hadrian*'s author by A.J.A. Symons that's unlike any other literary biography. Many writers have tried to imitate it without success. *Hadrian the Seventh* received little attention when it first appeared in 1904, and soon went out of print. It was Symons' book, first published in 1934, that made the novel and its author—who styled himself "Baron Corvo"—(in)famous.

Physical qualities matter when it comes to a book's stickiness in our lives. My copy of *The Quest for Corvo* is the blue Penguin paperback from the early 1940s with an advertisement for Greys Cigarettes, including illustration of a Yeoman of the Guard filling the back cover. "Just honest-to-goodness tobacco," the advert reads. Penguin Books had been recently founded, in 1935, revolutionizing books and publishing with their paperback format, soon-to-be-iconic bird logo, and innovative distribution (convincing druggists and grocers to stock books; sending paper books by pallet to the boys at the Front) techniques. In fact, the bird on my early 1940s *Quest* is in mid-stride. You'd have to see it to see what I mean. It's not the bird you know, or that your mother knew, on Penguins. This is also when Penguin Books was located in Harmondsworth, England—a city of no importance except that it was close to Heathrow Airport.

Normally a neurotic preserver of a book's original physical qualities, I've carried *The Quest* in the door of my Subaru every day of a Vermont winter, and left it overnight on the dock of our lake cabin in Wisconsin. At this point it is more like a worn wallet than a book, since I've bound the eighty-plus year-old paperback, which was printed on the cheapest of wartime paper, with tape in every possible way. I've carried it to places that recall how soldiers carried books in the trenches in the First War, or onto the beaches of France during the Second. We know, in fact, that at least 140,000 copies of this edition of *The Quest* were printed while Britain was at war with

Hitler, most of them carried in pockets into battle. We no longer treat books with such respect.

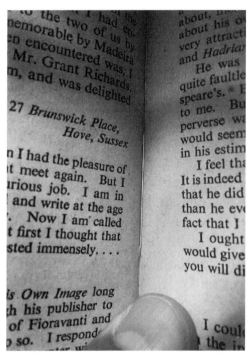

The fragile but sewn binding of my 1941 wartime Penguin

Not every page of my copy still has its back exposed to what originally glued it all together in the binding. Those free pages are where I have lingered particularly long with a cracking paperback while eating dinner alone at a bar, or elbow-to-elbow with other passengers on a subway train. Charles Lamb once loaned a copy of Milton to his friend Samuel Taylor Coleridge, saying, "If you find certain parts dirtied and soiled with a crumb of right Gloucester blacked in the candle (my usual supper), or peradventure a stray ash of tobacco wafted into the crevices, look to that passage more especially: depend upon it, it contains good matter." I can relate to this. Please bury me with this book.

Frederick Rolfe was a satirist par excellence. He saw the vices of the Roman Catholic Church close-up, and set out to ridicule it, and them. There was nothing unsullied about his satire, however, because Rolfe's own wickedness was rife in living detail, and is reflected on nearly every page of *Hadrian the Seventh*, particularly given Symons' revelations in *The Quest for Corvo*. Rolfe wrote from his obsession—again, with the mysterious and sometimes wicked Catholic Church—and in that quest, too, I can relate. Of course he was a convert; who but converts care so much about faith?

But Rolfe was also a traditionalist and an Italophile. Several months spent as a guest of a wealthy English duchess in Rome— after being forcibly removed from Pontifical Scots College, the second seminary which asked him to leave—led to him affectatiously adopting the *nom de plume*, the very character, of Baron Corvo. He would never again be allowed to pursue Roman Catholic holy orders, but his mind burned with that desire so much that he convinced himself he was better than any priest and smarter than any doctor of theology.

His certainties pour onto the pages of his books, and they are deliciously insecure. The spurned seminarian, for instance, turns his unrequited love into a defense of clericalism. For example, the narrative voice of *Hadrian the Seventh* (which is unmistakably Rolfe's own) describes the wonder some laypeople had for the new pope's holiness because "never had [they] heard anything so edifying" as descriptions "of the Holy Father's former predilection for white flannel shirts, white knitted socks and night-caps. They thought it heavenly of Him to have refused to wear any colours but white or black while He was living in the world." How quaint this way of revering a priest seems to Catholics today—except for many of the young men studying to become priests, who still seem drawn to such power.

I happened upon my copy of the novel in the compact, cluttered, and captivating aisles of Ann Arbor, Michigan's Dawn

Treader Book Shop. I was there to visit the corporate offices of Borders Bookstores on East Liberty, just across the street. It was the late spring of 1995. All I brought with me for the appointment was the required paperwork and a bag full of samples and galleys that I planned to give to the corporate book buyers with whom I was about to meet. Sitting in the waiting room were real suit types, holding cardboard cutouts and other accoutrements of "book dump" displays they intended to pitch to these influential buyers. All of the suits were in pairs or threes; apparently, a single hustler with a catalog and some books was not enough. Well, that was me. The air wreaked of cologne.

I was mostly interested in the list of used bookstores in my back pocket, to which I'd turn immediately after my meetings were done. Dawn Treader was at the top, for good reason, I discovered an hour later, and near the front desk and cash register, where 1920s and '30s Modern Library and Phoenix Library hardcovers were lovingly displayed, *Hadrian the Seventh* called to me. It had no jacket, and was the 1929 Chatto edition, rather than the first edition published a quarter century earlier. I've seen a few copies of that one available for $7,000 or so since. Needless to say, I've never purchased one. Never mind; you always love your first. There are a couple of jacketed 1929 copies on my shelves now, but it's the first one I found with stains on the red front cover that remains in my shoulder bag much of the time.

Every novel has an agenda, novels about popes perhaps more than most. It is said that Anthony Burgess's papal novel, *Earthly Powers* (1980), was designed to make fun of Burgess's fellow novelist and rival, Somerset Maugham. Rolfe's *Hadrian the Seventh*, similarly, was written to settle scores. Self-indulgent to the core, written after he was kicked out of seminary, it is brilliant, self-delusional, autobiographical wish-fulfillment. If you know a bit of the author's biography, the combination of personal bitterness and comedy makes you laugh out loud. The hero is Rolfe himself, hardly veiled, and that hero is begged by bishops and cardinals appearing one day on his doorstep in London, admitting their mistakes for doubting his potential in the seminary, begging the still-young man to accept not only holy orders but eventually the Holy Pontiff's chair. As pope, he takes the name Hadrian in honor of the real Adrian IV, who remains the only Englishman ever elected (in 1154) pope. Rolfe Latinized the name to make it Hadrian and added the VII. In the novel, after turning the world upside down, the fictional Pope Hadrian dies from an assassin's bullet, all martyr, which is what Rolfe had been in real life from first to last.

When he wasn't styling himself as the inheritor of a barony, an entitled lord of the realm, Rolfe called himself "Fr. Rolfe," supposedly to indicate the Frederick of his forename, but actually as a tool for his imagined ordination to the priesthood. He also fussily used archaic words—such as "digladiator," "imperscrutable," "epistatai," and then "pachydermatosity" to describe a cardinal's public face. He wanted to demonstrate his superiority to everyone around him, including his readers. His called his preface, "Prooimion," ancient Greek for the same.

Then there are Rolfe's reveling in cat-like qualities: his hero purrs, demonstrates agility, and responds with feline "scratches" proudly and repeatedly. Every reform of the fictional Hadrian VII's papacy is tinged with revenge that not only could a rejected seminarian appreciate, but every writer who has received rejection slips from book publishers (Rolfe knew both of these things in real life). Did Rolfe also know that his namesake, Adrian IV, had once been rejected as a postulate at his local monastery in St Albans, outside London? As this new fictional pope settles down to write his first encyclical, he's reflecting...

> His memory flew back to the time when people used to jeer at Him for His habit of writing letters, letters which explained a great deal too much, to blind men who could

not see, to deaf adders who would not hear. He chuckled at the thought that those same people would read, mark, learn, and inwardly digest, every word and every dotted i of His letters now—letters which were not going to be painfully voluminously conscientiously persuasive any more: but dictatorial.

Even the routine capitalizing of the third person pronoun somehow reveals the grim, arrogant, vulnerable, delusional pain felt by this pope in ways that can't help but seem delicious and ridiculous. Hadrian VII is a Holy Father who despises not only the men who elected him but the people whom they represent. There's no pretense otherwise:

> As for the Faith, I found it comfortable. As for the Faithful, I found them intolerable.

My own fascination and unease with papal history and power drew me to Corvo's novel at first, and still. There are many features of the fictional Hadrian VII that pointed me to the earlier and very real Pope Celestine V, who in the late thirteenth century was plucked from obscurity, led to the papal palace, and installed almost against his will as the successor of St. Peter, to rule only briefly and tragically. Like Hadrian VII, Celestine V was destroyed by the Powers That Be. The papal curia despised them both. The faithful wondered about both, if they were saints or madmen. And both Hadrian VII and Celestine V were ahead of their time, for instance, Celestine's separation of worldly from spiritual authority in his pontificate, and Hadrian's canonization of Joan of Arc in his.

It was while I was carrying *Hadrian the Seventh* with intensity in the first decade of this century that I began also traveling to Rome and Naples to research the life of Celestine V, and then wrote my book about him. And it was at the end of one of those trips when a friend and I stood in St. Peter's Square and he asked me with a measure of exhaustion, "Why don't you just become a Catholic already?", that I finally did. I came home and, one week later, visited our local priest for the first of a dozen meetings to discuss all matters of faith and practice. And when that priest said to me in late summer, "I think you're ready. Did you have a day in mind when you'd most like to enter the Church?" I said that I knew that this year the feast of St. Francis of Assisi, October 4, fell on a Sunday, so how about then. He agreed. The friend with whom I'd traveled to Naples to see the castle where Celestine V lived, and the paintings of him on the walls, left his home in London once again that October to come to Vermont and stand as my sponsor.

Rolfe was also gay, and painfully so, since it was an era long before it was remotely safe to come out of the closet. Rolfe's personal story of intense desire for the priesthood, painful relationship breaks with other men, and when leaving behind his priestly fantasies substituting them with sexual promiscuity, all makes some sense when you read the literature about men and homosexuality and the repressiveness of the teaching of the Roman Catholic Church.

Corvo's influence is all over "The Young Pope," the HBO series from 2016 written and directed by Paolo Sorrentino. For instance, in the second half hour of the first episode, Sister Mary (played by Diane Keaton) lectures "Lenny," which is her name for the young, fictional Pius XIII (portrayed by Jude Law), since she raised him in an orphanage. She says: "Your personal aches, your enormous sufferings, your terrible memories—it's a harsh thing to say, Lenny, but I have to say it: they must take a back seat.... Now the time has come for you to let your sorrows fade, to become irrelevant, distant memories...overpowered by the terrible responsibility that God has given you." Lenny pays no heed to this. He lashes out, just as Baron Corvo's Hadrian VII did.

Rolfe died in Venice in October 1913, having traveled there in 1908 with a male archaeologist friend. He never left. The dream of the priesthood had vanished, so too did his pious personal oath of chastity, leaving him a tinderbox to seemingly every young male flame. He developed an inhibition of taking nude photographs of male friends and strangers, and these facts have led him to be championed by readers of forgotten gay writers. Even so, an interesting one-man play by Martin Foreman, "Now We Are Pope: Frederick Rolfe in Venice," dramatically imagines the final hour of Rolfe's life in Venice, portraying him at the end of his life—still bitter, ranting, disillusioned, miserable, confused—imagining that he is indeed pope, and the crowds in St. Peter's Square are cheering for him.

This author of my favorite book was also probably psychotically narcissistic. When he wrote the other work for which he's most often remembered, *Chronicles of the House of Borgia*, he came to see himself in the central figure of Rodrigo, of the famiglia Borgia, who became the corrupt and philandering Pope Alexander VI, reinterpreting him as innocent victim of others' deceits and circumstances, just like Rolfe himself.

Still, somehow, I end up seeing myself in Baron Corvo, as well as in the Corvo quest of A.J.A. Symons. I have my own inner fuel of petty animus; if I were talented enough, I'd pour them into a novel. Another favorite author of mine, Thomas Merton, once mused (like Edith Stein) in his private journal, "We are all secrets," and surely this is why so many of us read with ardor about other people and their all-too-transparent problems: to grasp ourselves.

CHAPTER 14

WITH PATIENCE LIKE SPRING AND THOREAU'S *JOURNAL*

LMOST FIVE YEARS into my marriage with Michal, she chose not to renew her contract at the local synagogue where she was serving in Ann Arbor, Michigan. She also did not yet want to find another congregational position. So we said to each other that Vermont felt like home, and to Vermont we returned.

We found a historic 1890s house on a small mountain just off downtown in Montpelier, a downslope of the city's Hubbard Park, directly opposite the downslope that leads to the State Capitol. It was a beautiful, scenic spot. Each year, the annual 4th of July parade saw the entire Vermont Congressional delegation—just three, including Senator Bernie Sanders—at the foot of our driveway, as the natural staging area for both floats and participants.

The public library was close at hand. Everything was close by. Montpelier is the smallest of state capitals, with only 8,000 people. The public library had one of those blessed collections that had not been culled and weeded according to twenty-first century principles of library science collection management. There were 1880s editions of Thomas Hardy novels on the shelves, and rare first edition volumes of Carl Sandburg's Abraham Lincoln biography on that beautiful hand-woven rag paper that seemed so appropriate to both subject matter and author. There were also first edition volumes of the *Journal* of Henry David Thoreau still on the circulating shelves.

One morning, while returning volume XII of Thoreau's *Journal* at the end of my checkout period, I decided not to place the much-battered book from 1906 into the wooden book return slot by the front desk, but instead to speak about it with the desk librarian.

"Good morning," I said.

She nodded, with a native New Englander's stoicism.

"I've checked out each of these Thoreau journal volumes and I'm delighted that you have them. They are wonderful. But as you can see [holding it up, for our mutual inspection], this one is coming apart on both the front and rear hinges."

She was looking, and seemed to take note, but did not speak. So I kept going.

"I wanted to urge someone to have this one repaired. It is very worth holding onto."

"Yes," she then said, vaguely.

"Please don't get rid of it. Such a valuable book. But it's falling apart," I concluded.

"Thank you," she replied. And without anything further, I left the volume in her hands. A good librarian is like a good physician, prepared to care for both body and soul.

Now—addict that I am—I was an almost daily visitor to the perpetual library sale in the basement of that building. And it so happened that on the following morning as I stopped by to look at the nonfiction tables I saw something surprising looking back at me. Sometimes there were new books put out in the mornings from an unknown stash of for-sale-ables held somewhere in the recesses of the old building. There on the table I saw Thoreau's *Journal*, volume XII, without any repair whatsoever, but instead with a very rude and fresh "DISCARDED" stamp announced on the rear flyleaf.

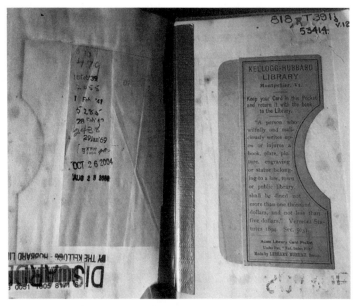

The discard stamp was used quickly and rudely.

"All hardcovers, $1," read the sign at the front of the library sale room, as usual. So I picked up the book, without inspecting, familiar as it was to me already, and handed the desk librarian a measly dollar on my way out, saying nothing further. My previous day's pleading had obviously gone unheard or unheeded.

Since that day, I have purchased other volumes from the old Houghton Mifflin series of the *Journal* from used and rare booksellers by mail, but none of them holds the allure that this first one-dollar copy has on me. When another volume arrives in the mail, I scrutinize its condition and lament every tiny fault in the physical object. But in my one-dollar volume I revel in the tears and the stains and the ugly tape.

My reading of Thoreau began years earlier, before moving to Vermont. I was living on the road and on planes, in rental cars and hotel rooms, selling books to booksellers, but wishing for another kind of life altogether. One night, to avoid evening paperwork while in Denver, Colorado, I left my hotel room to return to the four-story Tattered Cover Bookstore in Denver's Cherry Creek neighborhood where I'd been earlier that day. I was looking for something, I didn't know what.

The volumes of Thoreau's *Journal* were publishing then in Princeton University Press's "Writings of Henry David Thoreau" scholarly series, and starting that night it became my habit on trips to Denver to buy one every time. I'd carry the most recent in my shoulder bag each day until the next visit to the Tattered Cover, when the next one would replace it.

There were other books about Thoreau, and Thoreau's friends. On the road I would spend evenings in bookstores and libraries in the cities where I was traveling. I read everything that the Thoreau scholar, Robert Richardson, wrote about the period and its writers. I still remember the adrenaline rush when I opened Richardson's biography of Emerson for the first time, and then the sense of loss as that feeling left me in the early hours of the morning, since my mind returned to the hotel room and meetings for which I had to prepare.

We live in a time when reflection, and thoughtfulness generally, have trouble existing in words that are spoken out loud or written down. The racket, in a million places and by a million voices, makes it impossible to locate actual wisdom. And if wisdom happens to be spoken or written, it is destroyed within minutes by the din. I wonder, what is the value of reasoned and spiritual talk at such a time? But Thoreau showed a way forward. He's remembered as the one who lived intentionally, taking up residence at Walden Pond and writing the classic book you read in high school or college, *Walden*. It was first published in 1854. I'm not going to take you back to those pages, but to his journal pages, which are where all of his published writings began. It is Thoreau's *Journal* I carried, volume after volume, for a decade. He wrote there only for himself, to track his own simple life. It's a simplicity that I needed.

Thoreau's insights turned me around. They are particularly useful for an exhausted spiritual and religious person. Because we've read books, listened to great teachers, made changes in our lives, and then started again. We are the spiritually and religiously earnest and busy and tired. We often alternate between two poles of expression: an intensity of striving followed by an indifferent mystical assumption. *I must do this now* followed by *I am confident where I stand.* Neither pole gets us very far. We go in circles.

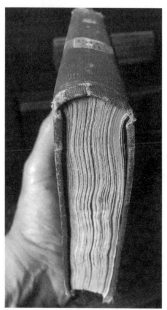

My battered 1906 Thoreau's *Journal* volume.

Thoreau's vision is quietly steady, consistently meaningful, taking into account the world as we experience it as well as the divine potential we desire for ourselves and the world: "I am of kin to the sod, and partake largely of its dull patience—in winter expecting the sun of spring," he reflected. This is the holiness of expectation. It is the counterpoint to the titillation of desire.

When I say that I carried the *Journal* volumes, I mean everywhere. One of them has infant spit-up on its dust jacket. Another was chewed by my cat. I even spilled spaghetti sauce on one of them one evening over dinner, then hurried to the restaurant bathroom, holding the book block so tightly—like I've never had to hold an arm or leg to avoid a hemorrhaging—wiping it as clean as I could under cold faucet water, allowing none to seep into the pages. These books were well-read, but they were talismans too.

Thoreau wrote as one in opposition to established faith, because his ways were unacceptable to the New England Puritans and Unitarian rationalists of his day. His church was entirely outdoors. "I am not offended by the odor of the skunk in passing by sacred places. I am invigorated rather," he wrote. But in the twenty-first century, his spirituality and practice are what people of faith like me often need. I'm trying to fill a vacuum left by the loss of meaning of sin, grace, and redemption, and Thoreau's practices of hope, patience, and gratitude are like pearls discovered in a field.

Bulgarian poet Janos Pilinzsky said, "I would like to write as if I had remained silent," revealing a contemplative approach to life inspired by Thoreau and so unlike my usual way of behaving. "God sees me standing in the sun," became one of Pilinzsky's late poems, and the passive relationship with God that the line implies, was deliberate. It doesn't mean that he felt alienated or alone, only that there was nothing much to be done. I often feel that Thoreau has quietly and steadily over the years become my antidote for what once was intense desire, intention, and penance, until I realized that these things really don't seem to move me any closer to what I seek.

To say it positively, I've come to realize how we live in a time when hope and patience are lost spiritual practices, and they need to be found. We live beyond the time when it makes sense to ask for God's blessing and then expect to receive it, as if manna still falls from the skies for hungry people. We still have preachers who hold onto this ancient language, and toss it like scraps to the starving, but for most everyone I know, it either no longer satisfies or doesn't satisfy for long. God simply doesn't work that way anymore.

So, we wait. And in our waiting, we share with sincere people everywhere hope and expectancy, rather than certainties. We are sure in our hope, that it is the meaning and purpose of our lives. For me, this is Christian. It is the way of Jesus in the Gospels. For a Jew it may be Jewish. For a Muslim it is Islamic. For a Lakota, it's Lakota. Waiting and hoping are also the ways of Tao. As Alan Watts wrote a half-century ago, the Taoist is to embody *wu-wei*, which means "non-action," and is, in his words, "going with the grain, rolling with the punch, swimming with the current."

So Thoreau carried me into the woods in ways that allowed me to finally understand such quiet, unambitious places. I hiked greater distances. I paid closer attention to plants, bugs, scat, trees and markings on trees, and I took note of the birds and mammals who were there with me. This attentiveness I learned from Thoreau's own note-taking, which is what fills so many pages of those *Journal* volumes. His was a native wisdom gleaned from the natural world. The natural world contains and sustains our lives; it and its rhythms are not just the environment of our living, but of our being. Take the decaying of leaves in autumn, for instance, of which Thoreau said in one of his final essays, "we are all the richer for their decay [that] prepares the virgin mould for future cornfields and forests, on which the earth fattens." This affected how I prayed and the fewer words I used to do it, since I began to see presence and attention itself as a prayer.

All these inspirations place high value on waiting and patience, and they have transformed how I approach my faith and practice. I spin and toil less than before, unconcerned about expectations and permissibility. I contemplate more, responding to the demand of my natural environment which says slow down and listen. Hope has largely replaced belief. These inspirations of waiting and patience are not a way of giving up religion—not at all—in fact, they expect a great deal of God or whatever word we use that means "God." I lean into Source, Spirit, Light, Darkness, Wind, Sun, Someone. If not attending church meant you were called an atheist in Thoreau's day, then so be it. He was unconcerned with such things, and wrote in his *Journal* of

> Reverently listening to the inner voice [without] a particle of will or whim mixed with it.

Waiting and patience place hope in the Divine's abiding presence and goodness. These are not ideals foreign to Christians, Jews, and other religious people, but they are often thwarted by the words and instructions of our catechetical traditions. Expecting the sun to rise again in the morning is the best phrase I can use to describe what I do now that's religious. It is a simple practice I learned from Thoreau's *Journal* that runs much deeper than faith, producing in me expectation of that grace that opens, still without fail, in my life again like spring flowers.

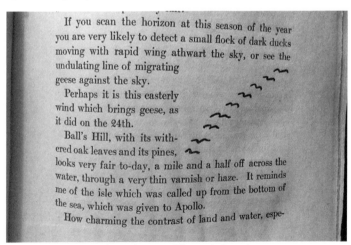

If you scan the horizon at this season of the year you are very likely to detect a small flock of dark ducks moving with rapid wing athwart the sky, or see the undulating line of migrating geese against the sky.

Perhaps it is this easterly wind which brings geese, as it did on the 24th.

Ball's Hill, with its withered oak leaves and its pines, looks very fair to-day, a mile and a half off across the water, through a very thin varnish or haze. It reminds me of the isle which was called up from the bottom of the sea, which was given to Apollo.

How charming the contrast of land and water, espe-

A sample page of Thoreau's *Journal*

CHAPTER 15

GHOST STORIES
AS KIDS GO OFF TO COLLEGE

N THREE-PLUS DECADES of parenting I have carried many books, mostly for me, but some also for my children. I'll always be grateful to Margret and H.A. Rey's *Curious George* franchise for creating such a dull rhythm of words, combined with smiling illustrations and a brilliantly identifiable character, such that my two-year-old son was able to finally sit still for ten minutes. That's why I was reading to him. I remember it as something like: *George wondered what was up there. So George began to climb. He climbed and climbed. Up and up he went until he stopped. Then George looked down. He had climbed so far!* As I wanted to toss the book out a window, there was my son Joseph sitting on the edge of his seat waiting for the delivery of the next dull line.

Also important for my little boy was *The Story of Ferdinand.* This was just after I was called to school to meet with the principal because Joe, in third grade, was once again caught hitting one of his classmates on the playground. Author/illustrator's Munro Leaf's portrayal of a bull in Spain, coaxed and prodded to become fierce and entertain the crowd in the famous bullfights, who doesn't really want to fight and that's just fine—was a lifesaver that year. We must have read *Ferdinand* every day for two or three months.

But I didn't carry those books the way that I have carried others, as if my life depended on them.

Joe's older sister, Clelia, left high school a year early, because her life was a mess at home—her mother and I were recently divorced, and frequently arguing—and since high school had turned out to be a big disappointment. She was a bookish kid—is still a bookish adult, now an adult services librarian in a college town in Iowa. One of her part-time jobs during high school was working in a used bookstore owned by a friend who was also her Suzuki-style piano instructor. For almost two years I paid for the lessons mostly with books from my library.

Miserable during sophomore year in high school, which then turned to junior year, she started talking about colleges in southern California. Three thousand miles away from home must have looked pretty good to her. So over spring break week we flew to Los Angeles and visited Pomona and Occidental. But L.A. was not for her. Then I tried to show her Emerson College in downtown Boston. We toured there, as well. Again no. But when she heard that starting college before finishing high school was something a person could do, that singular solution became the only school in her sights: Bard Early College in Great Barrington, Massachusetts, just down the road a few hours from where we were in Woodstock, Vermont. She'd found a place to escape, and danced off to college, so happy to get out of town.

It was there I found Yellow House Books on Main Street and *The Collected Ghost Stories of M.R. James.*

Stories of preternatural uncertainty were what would accompany me through such a period in my life. My beautiful eldest child leaving home too soon. James' love of the uncanny fit well: frightening aspects in everyday life and unexplained presences that a modern skeptical mind finds ways to justify. I also knew that he knew and loved the Bible, as I did. In fact, the other book that M.R. James (his friends called him "Monty") is known for had been in and out of my bag for more than a decade already: *The Apocryphal New Testament*, in the 1926 printing of the 1924 Oxford University Press edition. No one who studies the European Middle Ages, as I have for almost forty years, can ignore texts such as "Pseudo-Matthew" or "Protoevangelium"—and they're evocatively full of demons, spirits, strange miracles, and even stranger presences.

Monty's father was an evangelical Christian clergyman and I too grew up hearing evangelical sermons, reading the Bible assiduously, its ideas and imagery filling my imagination. So when I read that Monty said, "There was a time in my childhood when I thought that some night as I lay in bed I should be suddenly roused by a great sound of a trumpet, that I should run to the window and look out and see the whole sky split across and lit up with glaring flame"—I knew the allusions to passages in St. Paul's letters and the book of Revelation—because I too believed this at eight, ten, and fourteen, like I believed in my mother's love.

Then there were the settings of these ghost stories. The libraries and churches, where characters pursue their reading or collecting pursuits only to encounter ghastly spirit-like things, were supposed to be models of timelessness, where the world's concerns fall away. I'm just old-fashioned enough that such places remain this way, almost stubbornly, for me.

Then there's the mood of the stories that surrounded me. James' tales reveal fascination with saints and the occult, and those allusions didn't matter to me so much as the sense of otherness they conveyed. And beyond the actual content on the pages, there was a mood I was in while reading, and there was a spirit and disposition to my world in those days of feeling abandonment and change. As the Chilean novelist, Roberto Bolaño, once wrote about a book: "I even remember the color of the Mexican sky during the two days it took me to read" [it] For me, the mood and the color of the sky lasted about a year. What was frighteningly unfamiliar darkly illuminated this time for me.

It was the day of dropping off Clelia at college when I happened upon *The Collected Ghost Stories of M.R. James*. The book—regardless of its author or title—caught my attention spine-out on a high shelf because it was in the same kind of British brown wrapper as my *Apocryphal New Testament*—the sort that in the 1920s through 1940s was most often removed by the bookseller at the time of purchase as no longer necessary and tossed in the trash. I'll pick up and look at any book with a jacket in that paper; it could be about trout fishing, but I'd still open it up, examine the copyright information, lift the jacket gently off the spine, and breath in its plain odor. The book jacket originated for marketing and beautifying purposes, like the Renaissance-era silk or leather wrappings called *chemise* (technically, a woman's undergarment) used by the wealthy on precious religious books, or the clay jars in which the Dead Sea Scrolls were found—"as means to store and protect their contents."

So, yes, I was attracted first to its beauty in simplicity. It then brought a thrilling sensation when I saw what it was. I tucked it under my arm without a care for what it might cost. Not long ago, I posted a picture on social media of my two M.R. James volumes standing together on my dining room table and a friend replied, "Looks like a couple of bottles of good scotch!" He was right.

The publisher of this one was the great Edward Augustus Arnold, nephew of the poet and critic Matthew Arnold. After working for publisher Richard Bentley, who I remember for championing bizarre bestselling novelist Marie Corelli, then running a magazine for another English publishing legend, John Murray, Edward Arnold struck out on his own as Edward Arnold & Co. in 1890. He became E.M. Forster's publisher—and M.R. James'. The device he had drawn, of someone walking in a Renaissance-era surcoat (knee-length) while reading a large tome, spoke to aspirational me. I like how publisher devices have made a comeback in the last half-century on title pages, led by Alfred A. Knopf's oddly ubiquitous Borzoi (that's a dog breed). The surcoated gentleman in my 1949 printing of *The Collected Ghost Stories* is on the title page too.

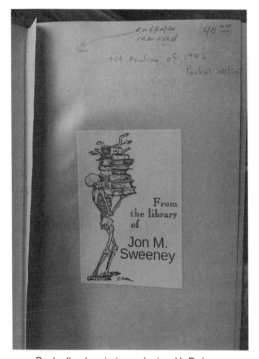

Bookseller description and price, M. R. James

I carried it throughout the fall and into the dark nights of a New England winter. The frights and eeriness were just what I needed. While also studying the habits of medieval monks at the Abbey of Cluny around this time, I happened upon the fact that abbots would attempt to correct misbehavior in their charges by telling ghost stories of dead monks returning in the night to give accounts of torments in the afterlife. In fact, according to the tenth-century *Life of Odo*, there was one monk who refused to observe the necessary silence in the monastery, and so first, "he lost his voice, the vehicle of his negligence. Three days later he died without ever speaking again."

An M.R. James ghost story asks, *Is the meaning of things answered by what you can see?* And the answer is no. The first of them is the only one I will describe here. It is the one that I reread multiple times that year: "Canon Alberic's Scrap-Book." The setting is a "decayed town" in the Pyrenees mountains where an Englishman with a penchant for medieval scholarship and ecclesiastical lore desires to spend a day making notes about and photographing every detail of its aged cathedral, St. Bertrand's. In fact, the anti-heroes of James' ghost stories are usually scholars of one sort of another, who are somewhat clueless about the world of space and time. In another story called "The Mezzotint" it's a curator in "pursuit of objects of art for the museum at Cambridge." In "Oh, Whistle, and I'll Come to You, My Lad" it's an aging professor of ontography—which is the study of how living creatures react to their physiographic environment—and that story is the only place where such a professor exists. Always these people are seeking small treasures, meaningful to only a few other people, and those treasures are most often found in books.

I get it. Several years before discovering M.R. James, I spent forty-eight hours in Nuremberg, Germany on my way to the Frankfurt Buchmesse in order to clock half a day each in two of its great churches, and to visit the city in which Albrecht Dürer was born and died. And just a year before finding *The Collected Ghost Stories of M. R. James* I spent a complete Sunday, from morning mass until candles after dusk, in Notre-Dame Cathedral in Paris; dinner alone on the sidewalk of a Montmartre bistro that evening marked the conclusion of a perfect day. In other words, this Englishman who asks a lonely sacristan (the little guy entrusted to care for the things in a church) to allow him access for several hours to things most people couldn't care less about, made perfect sense.

The monstrous elements in James' stories are at times Victorian (vampires) and other times Gothic (spiders). In "Canon Alberic's Scrap-Book," the sacristan appears "nervous" and "hunted." Here, there isn't anything monstrous, only inexplicable and other-worldly. The Englishman-scholar—his name is Dennistoun—and the sacristan are together alone in the great church, and after a couple hours the visitor encourages the sacristan to just leave him there. A chaperon is quite unnecessary. "You can lock me in if you like," Dennistoun says. "Good heavens!" exclaims the old sacristan, and there's a clear sense that to do such a thing would be either improper or somehow dangerous; the frightened old man insists on remaining.

As Dennistoun examines more artifacts—choir screen, stalls, organ, tapestries—there are occasionally troubling noises in the dark, cavernous, lonely space. Then there is what sounds like a distant laugh. The sacristan trembles but says everything is fine. There are also moments when the little old man seems to shake with fervor before certain religious objects—tears running down his cheeks, for instance—his reasons for crying still unclear.

By five p.m. it is dark. A winter's night. The sacristan appears more anxious than ever, and then grateful to see the tourist packing his things to go. Once outside, sacristan remarks to Dennistoun that he has a book at home—very close by—that may also be of interest. And when, a short while later, they arrive at the man's house, a large volume is produced from a chest in a private oratory, and only by standing on a chair to reach it: a "large folio," meaning a book from the early decades of the invention of the printing press, on large sheets, bound. This is Canon Alberic's scrap-book of the story's title.

The excitement of the find is palpable. Recounting everything that happened that night, Dennistoun begins to tell of some of the leaves, many of them stamped in gold, bound into that unique volume. Canon Alberic, whoever he was, had clearly plundered libraries to create it. "Here were ten leaves from a copy of Genesis illustrated with pictures, which could not be later than AD 700," Dennistoun offers. Then he adds how he was imagining doing whatever might be necessary to carry the artifact away from such a rural and forgotten place, back with him to the university at Cambridge.

The old sacristan's face is pale, watching the scholar with the book, before he says, "If monsieur will turn on to the end." So Dennistoun keeps turning, and commenting on each rare bit he sees, his enthusiasm only growing. But he hasn't yet made it to the end.

Instead, he purchases the book from the old sacristan for 250 French francs, and carries it back to his room in the hotel. It is there, all alone, when what began as a sepia image of a demon on a page of the strange volume, takes on a physical body on the table beside it. M.R. James relays about the calm and scholarly-detached Dennistoun: "He flew out of his chair with deadly, inconceivable terror."

I wish that I'd had some similar experience, in order to cathartically heal what was instead the slow dissolution of every certainty and confidence I had as a parent, the work of all those years. Terror was what I was experiencing, if only I could have felt it.

This is where someone first purchased my M.R. James, in 1949.

CHAPTER 16

BLACK ELK SPEAKS
AND THE MYSTERY OF RELIGIOUS IDENTITY

EVERY BOOK LOVER knows how the appeal of a particular book often has little to do with its ideas. Books have a feel, and they raise feelings in us. I think of the Marine at the start of Molly Manning's *When Books Went to War*, who while lying in bed fighting malaria is gifted an Armed Services Edition of *A Tree Grows in Brooklyn* and later credits that book, in a warm letter to its author, with helping him "feel more deeply than I did before." *A Tree Grows in Brooklyn* is a modern novel about the Nolan family, beautifully conceived and written, but ordinary in subject matter: family relationships and childhood dramas in the Williamsburg tenements. This Marine read that book over and over again. Left suffering and alone in a hospital bed, *A Tree Grows in Brooklyn* opened something inside him. "I can't explain the emotional reaction that took place," he wrote to novelist Betty Smith.

This is what *Black Elk Speaks* did to me, but without the drama of war or deadly disease. Nebraska poet John G. Neihardt's book about the Lakota sage and his lost way of life caused an "emotional reaction" in me—I'm going to steal the phrase because it is just right for what happened. Hopefully, every reader has had such an experience at least a few times in their lives. This is a story of one of mine.

After my first year of college—at an evangelical Bible school—I was sent by a conservative missionary society to join missionaries already in a rural province of the Philippines, attempting to convert Catholic Filipinos in order to have them rebaptized as Christian evangelicals. I'd raised the money to pay for my travel, asking relatives and friends and members of my church, anyone I could think of, and it worked, albeit the flights had to be as inexpensive as possible. So I flew from Chicago's O'Hare to Minneapolis/St. Paul, and from there to Seattle, from there to Seoul, then to Taipei, and from there into Manila. So more than twenty-four hours after waving goodbye to my parents at the gate I opened my blinkered eyes and looked for my hosts in the waiting area in the terminal. Then we drove the two hours south to Batangas City.

The dry season had hung on longer than normal, that year. It was hot and steamy, and the house had no air conditioning. The next morning, in desperate need of a shower, I discovered that we also had no hot water, but had to use a coil in a large bucket to make cold tap water warm enough to pour over our heads. I loved all of this. And most of all the people.

But there was a problem lurking behind all the appearances: In contrast to my missionary hosts, I no longer held that there was just one religious truth, and that I possessed it. And I was in a bit of crisis, not wanting to disappoint anyone, and without an idea of how to navigate my way into a way of life—religious, spiritual, and otherwise—that was more generous.

I remained in the Philippines for four months, a missionary failure of sorts, since I convinced no one to leave behind their faith or religion of origin. I was supposed to help with conversions, and I couldn't. With my study Bible and American white male over-confidence, I sat at the kitchen tables and in living rooms of Filipinos pretending that I knew everything; that I was there to explain to them the way of truth and life; but what happened was, they slowly converted me. A dozen of these intimate encounters later and I was asking more questions than I was answering. I wanted to know about the images of saints I saw all over their houses. I wanted to understand what was happening in the religious festival and parade I had witnessed in the center of town. I saw home altars for the first time. I asked my hosts how they prayed, and discovered it was both more often and very different from my own practice. Their indigenous Catholicism made me feel connected to God in ways that I had never felt before.

When I wasn't failing at my conversion tasks, I was starting a high school youth group, my other responsibility that summer. There were at least thirty kids coming to our meetings right away, mostly, I think, because they were curious to meet the American college student. I asked them what they would like to do together over the next twelve to fourteen weeks, and they'd clearly rehearsed an answer beforehand: put on a musical. So, pretending again that I knew what I was talking about, I went on to become the director of "Joseph and the Technicolor Dreamcoat." And by late August, we put on two performances. Each of the kids brought family and friends and it seemed to be a highlight for everyone in town. I left Batangas City with warm feelings for everyone I'd met, and with mountains of religious discomfort and spiritual confusion.

Books by Thomas Merton were in my suitcase and in my room in Batangas City throughout those months in the Philippines, as I mentioned in an earlier chapter. But it was *Black Elk Speaks* that I picked off a bookstore shelf the week I returned to the States, and its sense of loss and despair, hope and identity, spoke to me in ways that wouldn't have been possible just a few months earlier. I remember standing in the bookstore and reading the back cover copy, then flipping to the front of the book, quickly turning past the introduction and preface, which were written by other people, because I wanted to find the words of Black Elk himself. I read the opening paragraph: "My friend, I am going to tell you the story of my life, as you wish; and if it were only the story of my life I think I would not tell it."

I bought it, took it home, and read it slowly. Only about ten pages a day (I couldn't digest more than that at one time), for the next two weeks. Then, I read it again, and again. I've never met a person who was connected to other people, to animals and other created things, to the earth under his feet, and to the great spirit of all things surrounding him, as was the Black Elk I met in that book. He was attuned to listening and watching, but his frequent mystical visions both inspired and troubled him. To receive visions—beginning at a young age; for him they started at five—entailed great responsibility for his people.

He understood his enigmatic cousin, Crazy Horse, and how he was able to lead the Oglala Sioux to victory over Lt. Colonel George Custer and his Seventh Cavalry regiment at the Battle of Little Bighorn in 1876: "Crazy Horse dreamed and went into the world where there is nothing but the spirits of all things. That is the real world that is behind this one, and everything we see here is something like a shadow from that world. He was on his horse in that world, and the horse and himself on it and the trees and the grass and the stones and everything were made of spirit, and nothing was hard, and everything seemed to float."

Then, after recounting what he called his "great vision" experienced at age nine, Black Elk tells Neihardt of another mystical experience, which Neihardt records in chapter twenty-three: "Another vision came to me. I saw a Flaming Rainbow, like the one I had seen in my first great vision. Below the rainbow was a tepee made of cloud. Over me there was a spotted eagle soaring, and he said to me, 'Remember this.' That was all I saw and heard." And then: "I have thought much about this since, and I have thought that this was where I made my great mistake. I had had a very great vision, and I should have depended only upon that to guide me to the good. But I followed the lesser visions that had come to me while dancing on Wounded Knee Creek. The vision of the Flaming Rainbow was to warn me, maybe; and I did not understand.... It is hard to follow one great vision in this world of darkness and of many changing shadows. Among those shadows men get lost."

It would be twenty years before I would be introduced to a more complete portrait of Black Elk—the Lakota medicine man who was more than the person portrayed in Neihardt's great book—learning that he was also a convert to Catholicism who spent the second half of his life as a missionary and catechist (religious teacher). I would meet this Black Elk—and find that his full name was Nicholas Black Elk—twenty years later. And then a decade after that, I would write his biography. As someone who had once been a missionary myself, and also a convert to Catholicism, I was particularly drawn to how Nicholas Black Elk continued to hold more than one religious identity at a time. Conversion, for him, was new growth on a tree already well-formed. He was both all Lakota and all Catholic. For example, he learned to pray the Our Father, *Ateunyanpi* in Lakota, but his words for "Holy God," *Wakan Tanka* (literally "Great Spirit"), needed no change. Years later, his son, Benjamin Black Elk, put it this way: "Our pipe is older than Christianity.... My father was a Christian. He died a Catholic; he is buried in a Catholic cemetery. But he still believed the Indian religion." Somehow, across an enormous cultural divide, I understood.

I traveled to the Pine Ridge Reservation to see Nicholas Black Elk's grave for myself, and stood there feeling grateful to the Nebraska poet laureate for finding him and midwifing his story into existence. And to think that we simply stumble upon these books. Like a crack in the sidewalk, we fall headlong into them.

Browsing is a powerful thing. I wouldn't have found any of the books that have carried me without the curiosity, freedom, and availability of bookstore browsing. And to have success with finding what you didn't know you were looking for, is to learn how to browse more, and better, and with a seriousness that's almost religious in anticipation of discovery. Browsing is what my friend Jeff Deutsch calls "a form of rumination." One of the great booksellers of the last half-century, Jeff delineates several species of the human book browser, including "the *pilgrim*, seeking wisdom, they know not what or where, but knowing that they must find it; the *devotee*, who prays daily, regardless of the season; the *penitent*, who has not lived as they ought and is now seeking redemption, or at least forgiveness; the *palimpsest*, who reads and rereads and knows that every reading leaves its inscrutable mark."

Nicholas Black Elk showed me how a dual religious identity was possible. He gave me permission, at a time when I needed it, to hold seemingly contradictory views and practices in a single life.

If there is a continuum of fluid religious identities, at one extreme end might be the nineteenth century Bengali holy man, Ramakrishna (see chapter 9), who claimed to experience the Divine in a variety of religious-specific manifestations. In addition to his Advaita Vedanta and Vaishnava Bhakti devotions, he was also at times, he said, Christian, then Muslim, and so on. I haven't known many people who would claim something similar. At the other end of this spectrum of pluralists might be me, since I pray and worship and study with Jews more often than with Catholics, and yet I never describe myself as a little bit Jewish. I am no longer a stranger in a Jewish congregational setting (spiritually-speaking or literally), but I remain a frequent and knowledgeable guest.

But as Nicholas Black Elk knew so well, religions are mediated ways that we experience or express the Divine. For some of us, there are also unmediated experiences or expressions, and it is when these take place in less familiar religious places or congregations that we begin to move outside a singular religious identity. Thomas Merton—who remained a faithful Catholic, but curious about nearly every religious tradition he encountered—understood this. In his *Asian Journal* Merton wrote, "The contemplative life must provide an area, a space for liberty, of silence, in which possibilities are allowed to surface and new choices—beyond routine choice—become manifest." For him, this included contemplating a series of stone standing, sitting, and reclining Buddhas in India. "[L]ooking at these figures I was suddenly, almost forcibly jerked clean out of the habitual, half-tied vision of things, and an inner clearness, clarity, as if exploding from the rocks themselves, became evident and obvious," he wrote to his journal.

It makes sense that these experiences happen most often while praying or studying or praising in a religious setting that is unfamiliar. Sparks fly when we encounter Spirit outside the confines of where we usually contain it. This is why I wish unfamiliar religious confines on every person living. They lead to epiphanies and to moments of profound connection. My unscientific study tells me that people clearly rooted in one religious tradition, open to experiencing another, are more likely to find affinities for the other, than are those people who simply stay home. But be careful, then, not to offend anyone, not to overstep the lines, which are there for everyone's good.

We do not understand ourselves, let alone our reasons for something so complex and inner-woven as a religious and spiritual identity. I believe most of the time most of us unwittingly set about making ourselves vivid to others, in nearly every way. Then we imagine that this vividness is who we really are, and it's not. Nicholas Black Elk is on his way to sainthood in the Catholic Church. I imagine that he has figured this all out.

I also like how the Black theologian Howard Thurman once put it: "Always we are on the outside of our story, always we are beggars who seek entrance to the kingdom of our dwelling place. When we are admitted, the price that is exacted of us is the sealing of our lips." And then my Trappist monk friends who knew Merton personally sometimes say that there is a "no-name me" who I don't even know yet. Perhaps one day.

CHAPTER 17

MONTAIGNE'S *ESSAYS*
AND THE DEPENDABILITY OF CHANGE

HIS LAST STORY starts with throwing up. While in San Diego for one night, a dodgy-looking Mexican restaurant sat next to my hotel, and lacking the initiative to go farther afield after a long day of work, I ate what I know now were bad seafood enchiladas. Then I paid for it all night long in the bathroom. By dawn's early light, it was clear I had to postpone my return flight, and when I then wasn't leaving until the following evening, I had time to visit a bookstore I hadn't reached on bad enchilada day. There, my two-volume set of Montaigne sat grinning from a shelf.

I mentioned the philosopher Edith Stein in an earlier chapter, how she was satisfied with her life as a mystery. I'm going to return to that theme again in this last chapter, only now it is not just that we are mysteries to ourselves and others, but changing is perhaps more central to us than fixity. Montaigne wanted to make it clear that, after a lifetime of close examination, he realized he was not always moving forward. In fact, growing older wasn't about making linear progress at all. To paraphrase one of his famous lines—the winds of inspiration will move only sails of boats that are unmoored from shore.

As always, form matters. I'd passed by the French Renaissance philosopher for decades. Always, paintings of the author turned me off, as do most author photos on book jackets. Montaigne was a Renaissance writer, an apparently well-dressed one, which means you won't find an image of him without a fat starched and wired ruff around the neck, a tall balding head that makes him look like a Spanish soldier (or Ignatius of Loyola), and a nearly handlebar mustache. I'm as superficial as the next person, and for me, to see Montaigne the dandy is to avoid reading him altogether. So thank God for a book with an imageless author. It wasn't until I encountered a certain two-volume hardcover set in dust jackets, which also possessed just the right heft and no hype, that I was ready. I found it in San Diego on the shelves of a poorly-lit used bookseller who is sadly no longer there: Adams Avenue Book Store. I was dehydrated and woozy, a spirit made open and vulnerable by a body undone.

It mattered to me that the books had been previously owned and signed by a scholar of literature. He indicated where he'd purchased them—people used to do that on flyleaves—"Cambridge, October 1, 1932." So, his underlinings inside were meaningful: I selected the set, in part, for that reason. "Enriched with annotations, tripling their value," Charles Lamb once described books returned to him by Samuel Taylor Coleridge, and I've known the same pleasure.

Montaigne created the modern essay, and his interests ranged from conscience to cruelty to educating children and the motivations of cannibals. Also, prayer. Friendship. Experience. Solitude. How to die.

In his essay "Of Books," he tells us that he often forgets the author when he's reading; it's the ideas that matter. And if one book bores him, he'll stop reading and start another. Modern writers are of less interest to him than are the tried-and-true classics. I picked up from Montaigne the value of friendship with books. He enjoys them like a good friend or an excellent bottle of wine, for "companionship" on his life journey.

His essays progress haphazardly. The author keeps talking to himself, questioning himself. He has already written and published for many years when he begins the essay, "Of the Affection of Fathers for Their Children," by declaring that his whole writing project—the attempt to examine his life and life itself through writing—a "foolish undertaking" that was originally "brought about by the brooding solitude into which I was plunged." So much for the idea that silence and solitude are necessary for a writer, or that they always provide the clarity we need. I've known contemplative monks who were chattier and moodier than anyone I know raising children or heading to the office every day.

A few years later, after more essays—real classics, in fact—Montaigne writes of "finding myself empty and totally destitute of any other matter." He has nothing to teach anyone, no special knowledge, he says. But he decides to continue, saying that he will offer only "myself [himself] for the subject-matter.... So there is nothing noteworthy in this business but its oddness." This is what you'd have to call an underconfident man. Or an honest one.

It was this sobriety and realism that captured me in my fiftieth year and for five years after that. I carried my Montaigne volumes into some difficult moments, including a recent hospital procedure that is familiar to many.

The stuff you have to drink the night before a colonoscopy is truly disgusting—and, to make it worse, voluminous. I avoided this pleasure for as long as seemed reasonable. General practitioners start mentioning it in your late forties, and then more seriously when you hit fifty. A few years in a row, since I saw my doctor usually only once a year for an annual check-up, I got away with saying, "Right, I'll call the office and schedule that," and then never did. When I hit fifty-five, my smart doc stopped letting me slide.

It was my first serious medical procedure, by which I mean the first time I was administered anesthesia. I'd been lucky, and I'm grateful, but then I found myself, as they wheeled me in, contemplating death. I knew it was only a tiny possibility for one going under not to come back out, but then something interesting happened.

With a simple clarity, I realized, perhaps absurdly, that whether I woke up again to consciousness or not, I'd still believe in the Divine. Were I to find myself on the other side of a divide, aware of what was happening to me, never to see my loved ones, discovering that any sort of architecture of the afterlife was quite nonexistent, it would be okay. I would still know that the unknowable God exists and is somehow connected to me. Some way. I thought, as I was wheeled into the procedure room, counting down from ten, *I don't need Dante's dread descending-ascending circles of cosmic postmortem to see a life that endures beyond the grave.*

I wouldn't call this believing, or hoping, as we usually use those present participle verbs—as if to hope for the afterlife is the same activity as hoping it might rain this afternoon. The comparison would be apt only if I had spent my entire life preparing for, and looking for, this afternoon's potential rain.

But it is this kind of hope that I found in the essays of a Renaissance-era French writer who was simply trying to become a better human being. So this is a story about—I don't know—everything that matters. That's what Montaigne wrote about. It's ridiculous that we call him a "philosopher" on Wikipedia and Goodreads, and so on, because he doesn't resemble one in any way—not the Socrates kind, and certainly not the kind that you find in universities today. Montaigne was a writer through and through, and a reader over and over again. He knew how books answer questions, and not only didactically. We search and seek for answers to questions that will not go away with what we have found. And we find the books we need, whose authors speak for us what we haven't yet figured out how to say.

I want what Montaigne tells us he wants:

> In books I seek only pleasure through an honest pastime; or, if I study, I seek only the knowledge which tells me how to know myself, and teaches me to die well and to live well.

This gentle writer came to me at a time when I finally understood from experience how questions are better than answers, and that investigating truth is a lifetime affair.

A Catholic, he's not at all pious. In his essay "On Prayers" he wrote a half-millennium ago in ways that seem modern, seeing through the shows of piety that we make for others. "We pray as a matter of habit and custom," he says, which is why "I dislike seeing a man cross himself three times at the Benedicite, and as often at the Grace (and I dislike it the more as it is a sign I hold in reverence and continually use, even when I yawn." Then he admits, when most of us couldn't, the incongruity and disgrace that every other hour of the day he's likely involved in some form of "hatred, avarice, and injustice," concluding ironically: "What an amazing conscience that must be which can be at ease, whilst harboring under the same roof, in such peaceful and harmonious fellowship, both crime and judge!"

My AARP cards are beckoning. I keep tearing up their direct mail, but there will come a day, a time for that sort of resignation and planning. For now, I'm getting chickens, and planning to name them for famous chefs: Julia, Mary, Clare, Paula. I'm changing jobs. I'm bringing home too many rescue animals.

As I look back on much more than half a life, I see only that the progress I have made is in seeing that the road is rambling, wandering, and indirect. Destination and purpose come in the morning with gratitude and hope, and in the evening with thankfulness and anticipation. Long ago Montaigne was essaying that "petty ambitions," "cheap renown," and "strong passions" are all to be avoided, and "Of all the qualities of an excellent character patience is enough for us." That seems just right.

ALL THE REST
AND WHAT'S NEXT

LIZABETH HARDWICK PUBLISHED a short story in *The New Yorker* in December 1980 titled "The Bookseller." It tells of Roger, who owns a secondhand bookstore on Columbus Avenue on the Upper East Side of Manhattan. Roger doesn't involve himself much in the content of the books he talks about and occasionally sells to customers from his store. There's no question that "He is a man with a single overwhelming passion out of which his being flows," but "he does not *quite* read them." More subtly, Hardwick writes about this not-quite-reading that "there is no word accurate for his curious taking in" of the books that fill Roger's days.

There are many books that we talk about without carrying; there are also the many ones that we talk about without reading. For me, this list is much longer than those that I have brought fully into my life. There is only so much room, and time, and mind.

I think, for example, of William Blake. I have purchased more than a dozen editions of the complete writings, going back to college when my soon-to-be mother-in-law sent twenty dollars for my birthday and I walked into town to purchase the Blake Norton Critical. I must have carried it to my table at the campus evening hangout every evening, then, until the final weeks of senior year. But I never read very far or for very long.

Sometimes this is because the reading is stopped abruptly by the sparking of ideas it produces in the mind. This was Blake for me, at times. I've also been carrying around a cherry red paperback of the complete writings in the old Geoffrey Keynes edition published by Oxford University Press, reprinted multiple times in the 1960s and '70s, when I suspect a lot of young adults were pretending to be reading the poet. Ginsberg was quoting him. So were Bob Dylan and Ram Dass. The expanding consciousness and desired creativity of that generation—at least a decade older than me—made Blake part of the Age of Aquarius.

So I don't quite read him, but I also can't set him down. I write notes in my Blake editions. "Milosz called Blake an 'ecstatic pessimist,'" is jotted in pencil in my Keynes paperback. And I tear out paragraphs from articles about Blake, and keep icon cards that remind me of Blake illustrations, storing all of these in my copies. I also have the hardcover Keynes, published by the Nonesuch Library in London in 1961. There's nothing groovy at all about it. Looking inside while writing this chapter I found a ticket stub from a Notre Dame football game in 2013, and another ticket stub from the ferry that leaves Cheboygan, Michigan for Bois Blanc Island, where I spent summers as a child and young adult. I remember carrying this Blake to both places, and both times, I carried it more than read it.

I remember carrying it on that ferry ride because every time I go on a ferry now, I remember my only truly mystical experience, which took place on the boat to Bois Blanc Island in bad weather when I was twenty years old. Standing on deck alone—because everyone else refused to be in the rain and wind—I looked up at the sky with the opening lines from "The Marriage of Heaven and Hell" on my mind: "Rintrah roars & shakes his fires in the burden'd air; Hungry clouds swag on the deep." I still don't know what those lines mean, but I'm not convinced I need to; I saw the face of a prophet in the dark clouds above Lake Huron that day, and heard the roaring and shaking of God.

Then there is the question—always—*what's next?* When the writing of these chapters was done, for me, it was books of mystical poetry, and there have been many. We live in a ripe age for this need and these discoveries. It is a decade-old now, *Eating God: A Book of Bhakti Poetry*, edited by Arundhathi Subramaniam, but it found me only recently and I haven't yet let it out of my bag. We'll see if it carries me somewhere.

When I come to the end of this life, I think certain books will be left as a barometer of who I was, but they will sit on shelves quietly, with a private understanding. Ultimately, they have been useful to me alone, and when I am alone. They will mean little to anyone else. Of no particular rarity or measurable value, they will disperse to the winds, which is not what I hope happens to that other most useful and least revealing, yet uncreated, part of me.

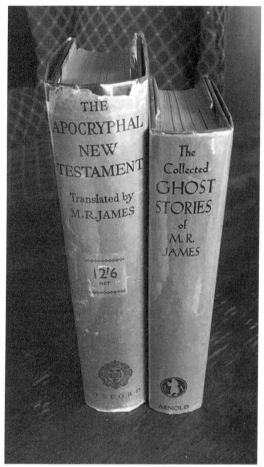

M. R. James books, like fine scotch bottles

ACKNOWLEDGMENTS

Thank you to Paul Cohen for seeing the value in this book and for his commitment to independent publishing for a quarter century. Monkfish gives me hope.

Thank you to the editors at *America* magazine, *The Christian Century*, and *Living City* magazine where a few of these essays saw an earlier life in forms that are much different than those in which they now appear. Similarly, a few paragraphs found in chapter 16 appeared first, differently, in my essay "Discerning a Dual Identity: A Case of Tightrope-Walking," in *With the Best of Intentions: Interreligious Missteps and Mistakes*, edited by Lucinda Moser, Elinor J. Pierce, and Or N. Rose. Thank you to Orbis Books for permission to adapt those paragraphs here.

Thank you to my wife, Michal, who always asks questions that challenge me, and from whom I will always have much to learn.

Thank you to my agent, Joseph Durepos, for offering a critique of a draft of the manuscript. And thank you to Mary Gordon, Jeff Deutsch, Richard Greene, and A.N. Wilson for kindly offering endorsements.

The dedication page speaks for itself, and my hope is that at least a handful of people will remember and share one of those memories with me.

SOURCES AND NOTES

Prologue

Victor Hugo, *Notre-Dame of Paris*, see the chapter, "This Will Kill That." "I hate to read new books" is William Hazlitt from "On Reading Old Books," first published in *New Monthly* magazine, London, 1821. R.H. Benson quote is from Donald Weeks, *Corvo* (London: Michael Joseph, 1971), 250. On David Swenson reading Kierkegaard, see *Something about Kierkegaard: Revised and Enlarged Edition*, by David F. Swenson, ed. Lillian Marvin Swenson (Minneapolis: Augsburg Publishing, 1945). I was alerted to Ralph Waldo Emerson's letter to Samuel Gray Ward by Jeff Deutsch in his *In Praise of Bookstores* (Princeton, NJ: Princeton University Press, 2022), 58. Lex Hixon, *Conversations in the Spirit: Lex Hixon's WBAI "In the Spirit" Interviews—A Chronicle of the Seventies Spiritual Revolution*, ed. Sheila Hixon (Rhinebeck, NY: Monkfish Book Publishing, 2016), 1-2. "Books are a uniquely portable magic," by Stephen King, *On Writing: A Memoir of the Craft* (New York: Scribner, 2010), 114.

Chapter 1: The Martin Buber Book I Carried While My Marriage Failed

A.N. Wilson, *Confessions: A Life of Failed Promises* (New York: Bloomsbury Continuum, 2022), 255. On neo-Hasidism and Buber see Arthur Green, preface, *Hasidic Spirituality for a New Era: The Religious Writings of Hillel Zeitlin*, ed. Arthur Green (New York: Paulist Press, 2012), xi-xii.

Chapter 2: Three Inches of Hitler in Very Small Hands

Nicolas Berdyaev, *Solitude and Society* (London: Geoffrey Bles, 1938), 115. Iris Murdoch, "The world is…" is from *The Black Prince* (New York: Penguin Classics, 2003), 340.

Chapter 3: *A Means of Escape* with My Side of the Mountain

"Bookhood," from Emma Smith's *Portable Magic: A History of Books and Their Readers* (New York: Alfred A. Knopf, 2022), 12; and "form matters," ibid, 10. Jean-Luc Nancy, *On the Commerce of Thinking: On Books and Bookstores*, trans. David Wills (New York: Fordham University Press, 2009), 16, 17-18. "Tylenol bottle purchased from a grocery in downtown Wheaton"—see the recent investigative reporting series of the *Chicago Tribune* on this unsolved crime, in particular "Tragedy, then Triumph: How Johnson & Johnson made sure its bestselling brand survived," by Stacy St. Clair and Christy Gutowski, *Chicago Tribune*, Section 1, October 28, 2022, 9. Walt Whitman, from "Give Me the Splendid Silent Sun," 1867.

Chapter 4: Forbidden Books for Ordinary Teenage Trauma

"Cardinal Newman's phrase": John Henry Newman, *Apologia pro Vita Sua*, ed. Martin J. Svaglic (New York: Oxford University Press, 1967), 15. "Young Rimbaud's phrases"—what follows are roughly lifted from the opening lines of *A Season in Hell*, in Arthur Rimbaud, *A Season in Hell and The Drunken Boat*, trans. Louise Varese (New York: New Directions, 1961), 3.

Chapter 5: In Search of Wendell Berry and a Life without Expectations

Photographs taken by Ralph Eugene Meatyard, *Father Louie: Photographs of Thomas Merton* (New York: Timken Publishing, 1991). I was so taken by those photographs that I wrote a poem about them, which became one of my first published writings: Jonathan Sweeney, "Lines on Gene and Father Louie," *The Merton Seasonal*, Fall 1991, vol. 16, no. 4, 24.

Chapter 6: Monica Furlong's Thomas Merton and How to Ruin a Honeymoon

Charles Lamb, from "A Quakers' Meeting," an Elia essay, 1821. M.F.K. Fisher, see *Gastronomical Me* (New York: Duell, Sloan & Pearce, 1943). "By this time…" Thomas Merton, *The Seven Storey Mountain* (New York: HarperOne, 1999), 410.

Chapter 7: Finding Tagore in Harvard Square

"Those who love life do not read…" is Michel Houellebecq from *H.P. Lovecraft: Against the World, Against Life*, quoted by Rob Doyle in

Autobibliography (London: Swift Press, 2021), 1. Poems, *Rabindranath Tagore*, mine is the 2nd edition (Calcutta: Visva-Bharati, 1943). Tagore's best biographer: *Krishna Kripalani, Rabindranath Tagore: A Biography, Second Revised Edition* (Calcutta: Visva-Bharati, 1980); my copy is inscribed "Students of the Department of Philosophy, Rabindra Bharati University, Calcutta, December 22, 1987" to "Lady Strawson and Professor Sir P.F. Strawson." Aurobindo Bose's suggestion is in the introduction to *Lipika*, by Rabindranath Tagore, trans. Aurobindo Bose (New Delhi: Rupa & Company, 2002), 9. On Tagore writing to Ezra Pound from 1000 Massachusetts Avenue, see *Rabindranath Tagore: An Anthology*, eds. Krishna Dutta and Andrew Robinson (London: Picador, 1999), 157. "Counterfeit truth" critic: Annette R. Federico, *Idol of Suburbia: Marie Corelli and Late-Victorian Literary Culture* (Charlottesville, VA: University Press of Virginia, 2000), 33. Tagore 1912 letter "such a dismal city," quoted in *Rabindranath Tagore: A Biography*, by Krishna Kripalani (Calcutta: Visva-Bharati, 1980), 83. Tagore letter to C.F. Andrews, in *Friendships of "Largeness and Freedom": Andrews, Tagore, and Gandhi, An Epistolary Account 1912-1940*, ed. Uma Das Gupta (New Delhi: Oxford University Press, 2018), 12. "Radice was determined": see Martin Kampchen, ed., *Gitanjali Reborn: William Radice's Writings on Rabindranath Tagore* (New Delhi: Social Science Press, 2017), 40.

Chapter 8: Tolstoy's Twenty-three Tales *and Learning to Walk on Water*
George MacDonald, from the 1893 essay, "The Fantastic Imagination." Tolstoy quotes: "I believe in God," from *On Life and Essays on Religion*, trans. Alymer Maude (New York: Oxford University Press, 1959), 223; "What do I care" quoted by John Givens in "Tolstoy's Jesus versus Dostoevsky's Christ: A Tale of Two Christologies," 15, from the "From Russia with Love" conference at Rochester Institute of Technology; "God is for me"— the opening sentences of "Thoughts on God," in *My Religion; On Life; Thoughts on God; On the Meaning of Life*, trans. Leo Wiener (Boston: Dana Estes and Company, 1904), 409; "As soon as man applies his intelligence," journal entry of March 12, 1870, quoted in *Tolstoy*, by Henri Troyat, trans. by Nancy Amphoux (New York: Penguin Books, 1970), 524; "If Christian teaching..."—unmailed letter written to L.Y. Obolensky, April 1885, see *Tolstoy's Letters, Volume II: 1880-1910*, ed. and trans. R.F. Christian (New

York: Charles Scribner's Sons, 1978), 381. The complete "The Three Hermits" is in Leo Tolstoy, *Twenty-three Tales*, trans. by Mr. and Mrs. Alymer Maude (that's how it reads on the title page) (Oxford, UK: Oxford University Press, 1903), 193-201. Paul L. Holmer quote from "Saying and Showing," lecture one, The Annual David Nyvall Lectures at North Park Theological Seminary, Chicago, IL, 1974; unpublished manuscript.

Chapter 9: Sitting with Swami and The Gospel of Sri Ramakrishna
Verrier Elwin, see for instance his *Leaves from the Jungle: Life in a Gond Village, 2nd edition* (Delhi: Oxford University Press, 1991), x-xii, 43-45, etc. Andrew Harvey's compilation is *Selections from The Gospel of Sri Ramakrishna: Annotated and Explained* (Woodstock, VT: SkyLight Paths Publishing, 2002).

Chapter 10: Hand-held Devotion (Books with Pictures)
"I wandered among its…—Tagore quoted in *Rabindranath Tagore: The Myriad-minded Man*, by Krishna Dutta and Andrew Robinson (New Delhi: Rupa and Co., 2000). 65. On Dürer's successful lawsuits, see "Fine art for God and Mammon," by Laura Gascoigne, *The Tablet*, thetablet. co.uk, February 11, 2023, 18. "Updike said…"—John Updike, "Dürer and Christ," *The New York Review of Books*, November 2, 2000; 17. Maximilian I's teeth: see Heiko A. Oberman, *Luther: Man Between God and the Devil* (New Haven, CT: Yale University Press, 1992), 26. Thomas Merton, *Seeds of Contemplation* (Norfolk, CT: New Directions, 1949). 93; this is the Merton book, in its original edition, with the unique burlap wrap around the boards.

Chapter 11: Sin and Mercy at Brighton Rock
"Faith. To believe" from Weil's notebooks, in *Simone Weil: Essential Writings*, ed. Eric O. Springsted (Maryknoll, NY: Orbis Books, 1998), 111-12. Graham Greene, "Simone Weil," originally in *New Statesman and Nation*, October 6, 1951, in his *Collected Essays* (London: Bodley Head, 1969). "It's not what you do," Graham Greene, *Brighton Rock: An Entertainment* (Middlesex, UK: Penguin Books, 1968), 128. A few chapters later… *Brighton Rock*, 166. "I'm one," Ibid, 53-54. "I went to church," Ibid, 168-69.

Chapter 12: A Tiny Volume of What's Impossible

Richard Crashaw, "On a prayer book sent to Mrs. M.R.," lines 17-20; I've modernized spellings. Library carrels like monastic cells, see Jason Camlot's "Introduction: Private, Public, and Personal Libraries in Situ and in Circulation," in eds. Jason Camlot and J.A. Weingarten, *Unpacking the Personal Library: The Public and Private Life of Books* (Waterloo, ON: Wilfrid Laurier University Press, 2022). Apprenticeship agreement, "his Secrets keep" etc. is from Daisy Hay, *Dinner with Joseph Johnson: Books and Friendship in a Revolutionary Age* (Princeton: Princeton University Press, 2022), 15. "Unfortunately, Sabatier's"—Neslihan Senocak, *The Poor and the Perfect: The Rise of Learning in the Franciscan Order, 1209-1310* (Ithaca, NY: Cornell University Press, 2012), 12; see pp. 4-16 for Senocak's full discussion of the Sabatier interpretation and influence. "Who you are" and "Who you should be," see *"Speculum*: Form and Function in the *Mirror of Perfection*," by Daniel T. Michaels in *Francis of Assisi: History, Hagiography and Hermeneutics in the Early Documents*, eds. Jay M. Hammond (New Hyde, NY: New City Press, 2004); 250-63, especially 253. Collections from Zen and Confucian traditions: see *The Twenty-four Filial Exemplars* and *Crazy Cloud Anthology* (different editions).

Chapter 13: Carrying Baron Corvo and My Own Petty Animus

William Hazlitt, op cit. Charles Lamb letter to Coleridge, November 4, 1802. Nephew of Edith Stein (Ernst Ludwig Biberstein): "That was to us a dark" quoted in *Aunt Edith: The Jewish Heritage of a Catholic Saint*, by Susanne M. Batzdorff (Springfield, IL: Templegate Publishers, 1998), 120. "140,000 copies," see Robert Scoble, *The Corvo Cult: The History of an Obsession* (London: Strange Attractor Press, 2014), 315. Reference to my book about Celestine V: *The Pope Who Quit: A True Medieval Tale of Mystery, Death, and Salvation* (New York: Image Books, 2012); a year after *The Pope Who Quit* was published, Benedict XVI announced he was quitting and I was briefly in demand on television talking about when and why popes quit. Playwright Martin Foreman's "Now We Are Pope: Frederick Rolfe in Venice" was first produced in 2014 in London and Edinburgh, UK.

Chapter 14: With Patience Like Spring and Thoreau's Journal

Alan Watts, from *Tao: The Watercourse Way*. Thoreau, "we are all the richer" from "Autumnal Tints," a late essay, first published in 1862. Thoreau in a very early essay—from "A Natural History of Massachusetts." "I am of kin to the sod" is Thoreau, from a letter, May 2, 1848. Janos Pilinzsky, quoted in Elaine Feinstein's *Ted Hughes: The Life of a Poet* (New York: W.W. Norton, 2003), 202; Hughes translated and introduced Pilinzsky's poems. "I am not offended..." Thoreau, *Journal*, spring 1850. "Reverently listening" Thoreau, *Journal, Vol. 1*, eds. Bradford Torrey and Francis H. Allen (Boston: Houghton Mifflin and Company, 1906), 177.

Chapter 15: Darkness and Ghosts as Kids Go Off to College

"There was a time," a sermon of James' preached in 1933, quoted in M.R. James, *Casting the Runes and Other Ghost Stories*, ed. Michael Cox (New York: Oxford University Press, 1987), xii—but Cox mistakenly refers to these as "stark Old Testament concepts of accountability and retribution." Roberto Bolaño, *Between Parentheses: Essays, Articles and Speeches, 1998-2003* (New York: New Directions, 2011), 249. On publisher's devices, as for all wisdom on the physical qualities of books, see the bible, *ABC for Book Collectors, Fifth Edition, Revised*, John Carter (New York: Alfred A. Knopf (complete with Borzoi), 1991), 74-75. Dust jackets "as means to store and protect their contents," see Margit J. Smith, "The dust-jacket considered," CeROArt (OpenEdition Journals), September 2014, creativecommons. org. Abbey of Cluny and *Life of Odo*: see Scott G. Bruce, *Silence and Sign Language in Medieval Monasticism: The Cluniac Tradition c. 900-1200* (New York: Cambridge University Press, 2007), 46, 50.

Chapter 16: Black Elk Speaks and the Mystery of Religious Identity

Marine writing to Betsy Smith: In *When Books Went to War: The Stories that Helped Us Win World War II*, Molly Guptill Manning (New York: Mariner Books, 2015), xi. "My friend" is Black Elk in John G. Neihardt, *Black Elk Speaks: Being the Life Story of a Holy Man of the Oglala Sioux* (Lincoln, NE: Bison Books/University of Nebraska Press, 1988), 1. "Crazy Horse dreamed" Ibid, 53. Black Elk in chapter twenty-three: *Black Elk Speaks*, 249-50. "Our pipe is older"—Benjamin Black Elk, in *Black Elk Lives: Conversations with the Black Elk Family*, eds. Hilda Neihardt and Lori

Utecht (Lincoln, NE: University of Nebraska Press, 2003), 18. Jeff Deutsch, *In Praise of Good Bookstores* (Princeton, NJ: Princeton University Press, 2022), 25-26. Howard Thurman, *With Head and Heart: The Autobiography of Howard Thurman* (New York: Mariner Books, 1981), 270. Thomas Merton, *The Asian Journal of Thomas Merton*, eds. Naomi Burton, Brother Patrick Hart, James Laughlin (New York: New Directions, 1975), 117, 233-35.

Chapter 17: Montaigne's Essays *and the Dependability of Change*

"In books I seek only" Montaigne, "Of Books," in *Montaigne's Essays, Vol. 1*, trans. E.J. Trechmann (New York: Oxford University Press, 1927), 399. "We pray as a matter of habit and custom" Montaigne, "Of Prayers," *Montaigne's Essays, Vol. 1*, 309. "Enriched with annotations" Charles Lamb, from "The Two Races of Men," an Elia essay, 1820. Regarding present participle verbs, I am indebted to the late Paul L. Holmer for helping me understand language, believing, and hoping in this way. "Of all the qualities" etc. Montaigne, "Of Husbanding One's Will," in *Montaigne's Essays, Vol. 2*, trans. E.J. Trechmann (New York: Oxford University Press, 1927), 480.

Afterword: All the Rest and What's Next

Elizabeth Hardwick, "The Bookseller," *The New Yorker*, December 15, 1980, 38-45. These quotes are all from 38.

ABOUT THE AUTHOR

Jon M. Sweeney is an award-winning author who has been inter-
viewed in print by a range of publications from the *Dallas Morning
News* to *The Irish Catholic*, and on television for CBS Saturday
Morning and many other programs.

His book, *The Pope Who Quit*, (Doubleday/Image) was optioned
by HBO. *New York Times* Best-selling author James Martin, SJ, said
about it: "The tale, as exciting and compelling as any novel or film, is
beautifully told by Jon Sweeney. This long-forgotten saga is rightly
restored to its place as one of the most unusual episodes in the entire
history of the church."

Sweeney is also the author of forty other books on spirituality,
mysticism, and religion, including the best-seller, *Meister Eckhart's
Book of the Heart*, coauthored with Mark S. Burrows (Hampton
Roads), the biography *Nicholas Black Elk: Medicine Man, Catechist,
Saint* (Liturgical Press), and *Thomas Merton: An Introduction to His*

Life and Practices (St. Martin's Essentials and Penguin Random House Audio, 2021).

His bookish reputation is nothing new. In 2014, *Publishers Weekly* featured Jon in an interview titled, "A Life in Books and On the Move." He's worked in books and publishing since 1990. He began that decade as a theological bookseller in Cambridge, Massachusetts, and ended it cofounding a multifaith publishing house, SkyLight Paths Publishing, in Woodstock, Vermont. Today, he writes, reviews, edits, and recommends books. He is contributing editor for books at SpiritualityandPractice.com; editor of *Living City* magazine, published by Focolare Media in North America; codirector with his wife of The Lux Center for Catholic-Jewish Studies in Franklin, Wisconsin; and religion editor/associate publisher at Monkfish.

Jon speaks regularly at literary and religious conferences, is a Catholic married to a rabbi, and is active on social media (Twitter @jonmsweeney; Facebook jonmsweeney). He lives in Milwaukee's Upper East Side.

INDEX